"This book is a rich and intriguing reading delight. I loved it!"

Caroline Myss, Ph.D., best-selling author of *Sacred Contracts, Anatomy of the Spirit* and *Why People Don't Heal and How They Can.*

It is a book that will help anyone who reads it realize that God is a loving God of all people regardless of their background, religion or race. Further, from example after example given in these pages, Todeschi shows that this God will come to us through many different ways—when we are facing death, or financial or emotional trials beyond our ability to handle by ourselves—when we sincerely seek His help. I highly recommend it to everyone who is looking for proof of the love and caring of a universal God."

George G. Ritchie, Jr., M.D.
Author of *Return from Tomorrow* and *My Life After Dying*

"This book is a valuable contribution to the present need for specific and practical information helpful for leading an authentic religious life. The author gives an abundance of material from a wide variety of sources showing that persons of every kind of background and environment, in large numbers, are experiencing divine guidance and enabling power to overcome obstacles both within and without, both personal and social."

Richard H. Drummond, Ph.D.
Retired professor, comparative religions and ecumenical mission and history of religions. Author of *Toward a New Age in Christian Theology, Islam for the Western Mind,* and *A Broader Vision: Perspectives on the Buddha and the Christ*

Selected Titles by Kevin J. Todeschi

Dream Images and Symbols

Edgar Cayce on the Akashic Records

Edgar Cayce on Soul Mates

Edgar Cayce on Vibrations

Family Karma

One Woman's Century

Soul Signs

God in Real Life

Personal Encounters with the Divine

Kevin J. Todeschi

4th Dimension Press ■ Virginia Beach ■ Virginia

3rd Printing, April 2010

Printed in the U.S.A.

4th Dimension Press
215 67th Street
Virginia Beach, VA 23451-2061

ISBN 978-0-87604-584-8 (trade pbk.)

4th Dimension Press is an Imprint of A.R.E. Press

Cover design by Christine Fulcher

To Mary D. Stephens, (1914-2004)
whose love often bore witness to the very possibility
of bringing Heaven into the earth

"We are so captivated by and entangled in our subjective consciousness that we have forgotten the age-old fact that God speaks chiefly through visions and dreams."

Carl Jung

Contents

Introduction

Marcia Evans was at her wit's end. Depressed, scared and under more pressure than she believed she could deal with, Marcia couldn't help but wonder whether or not she was doing the right thing. Married since the age of nineteen, she was now thirty-seven, a college dropout, the mother of two teenage children and involved in a miserable relationship. Her husband was extremely controlling, filled with anger, verbally abusive and was known to become physically violent. He ran her life and their children's lives and expected total obedience. He scrutinized their every activity and conversation and forbade any discussion about God or spiritual beliefs in the home so that the children's minds "wouldn't be poisoned." Even though she did not know where to go or how to support herself and the children, Marcia had come to the inevitable conclusion that divorce was her only means of survival.

Her marriage had always been challenging, but in recent years it had deteriorated to the point where she was totally dominated by a man whom she no longer recognized as the boy she had married. Yet, in spite of the fact that all evidence confirmed divorce was her proper course of action, her personal fears, her husband's threats and fits of rage, and her worries regarding the children's welfare all made Marcia repeatedly question her decision. When she finally found the nerve to separate from her husband, he threatened her with court battles and accusations of adultery; Marcia's anxieties only increased. Sometimes by day she felt certain that she was doing the right thing. At night, however, when she was alone, she couldn't help but wonder whether she was making a mistake. Caught up in an endless cycle of indecision, Marcia felt as though she were going to explode from the pressure.

One night just before the court battle regarding her divorce had gotten underway, Marcia was awakened about 2:00 a.m. by the presence of man in her bedroom. She was lying on her stomach, alone in bed, when she felt someone awaken her. With the awareness of the presence came a feeling of complete peace and reassurance. Even though Marcia did not consider herself to be a religious person—after all, she had not attended the Methodist Church since being a teenager—Marcia knew beyond any doubt that the man standing in her room was Jesus. Suddenly, she felt the Presence climb into bed with her:

> He started to hug me. I felt his arms crossing over my chest and stomach. I could feel his chest on my back, his head slightly askew of my own. This hug was not tight but gentle. It was not sexual but reassuring. I could not turn to see him, but his arms looked and felt as solid as anyone who is alive . . . He held me silently for about fifteen minutes and then faded away.

When she got up the next morning, Marcia had the encouragement she needed to continue with her decision. As a result, she moved ahead with the divorce and somehow survived her husband's threats, his anger, the court battles and the many months of verbal abuse that followed. During her periods of greatest stress, she used her memory of the encounter to help her through all of the problems and difficulties: "I could envision that Christ was still with me, even when my ex-husband was screaming at me about some aspect of the divorce."

Today, Marcia is happy, self-certain, well adjusted and the owner of her own business. She has remarried and now has a husband who is kind, loving and truly supportive of her. Her life and her perception of who and what she is has changed to such an extent that her marriage to her first husband seems like it was an entirely different life that happened to an entirely different person. Even today, more than fifteen years after the experience, Marcia vividly recalls the presence and remains certain that it was genuine. She is convinced that she encountered the Divine just when she needed someone or something beyond herself to reassure her that she was doing the right thing.

Surprising as it may sound, Marcia's account is not unique. In his groundbreaking 1923 classic, *Cosmic Consciousness: A Study in the Evolution of the Human Mind,* Dr. Richard Maurice Bucke detailed numerous accounts of mystical experiences that seemed to suggest the existence of a Divine consciousness just beyond the material world, supporting the hypothesis that humankind is ever-evolving in awareness. Throughout history, people from every imaginable background and religious experience have become convinced that they encountered the Presence of the Divine. Some call that presence *Jesus,* others *God,* others *Mohammed,* some *Buddha,* and still others suggest it was an experience with an angelic or divine being.

Before becoming a doctor, Bucke first supported himself through a variety of careers and period adventures, such as pioneer, railroad hand and gold miner. Dr. Bucke eventually went on to medical school and distinguished himself as a medical doctor, a professor, a scientist and a superintendent for a mental hospital.

Still in print decades after its publication, *Cosmic Consciousness* became a classic because it attempted to find evidence for the experiences of spiritual awareness while striving to examine these accounts beyond the confines of any particular religious dogma. In fact, Dr. Bucke became convinced that cosmic consciousness had little to do with an individual's specific religious background and in one example used the life of the Hindu philosopher Sri Ramakrishna Paramahansa (1836–1886) to illustrate how these experiences transcended religious boundaries.

Ramakrishna was born into a poor Brahmin family and experienced one of his first Divine encounters as a child while watching a flock of cranes in nature. Apparently, while observing the birds, Ramakrishna became aware of an all-pervading presence he called the Divine. That encounter and others led Ramakrishna to the firm belief that the Divine could be found and witnessed in everyone and everything. As an adult he would admit to having had visionary experiences with Jesus, the Buddha, and the Divine Mother. In time he became convinced that all religions were essentially teaching aspects of the same Divine reality, and he sought to embrace them as his own:

> What is most extraordinary, his religion was not confined to the worship of Hindu deities. For long days he subjected himself to various kinds of discipline to realize the Mohammedan idea of

all-powerful Allah. He let his beard grow, he fed on Moslem diet, he continually repeated sentences from the Koran. For Christ his reverence was deep and genuine. He bowed his head at the name of Jesus, honored the doctrine of his sonship, and once or twice attended Christian places of worship. He showed how it was possible to unify all the religions of the world by seeing what is good in each one of them, and by sincere reverence for every one who has suffered for the truth, for their faith in God and for their love of men. He left nothing in writing. His friends wrote some of his sayings. He did not desire to found a sect. Bucke, 313

An earlier example of cosmic consciousness is found in the life of Jakob Boehme (1575-1624), from the village of Alt-Seifenberg in Germany. Born to simple but honest peasant parents, Jakob spent much of his boyhood tending cattle. After a brief education that enabled him to read and write, he was apprenticed to a shoemaker. Serious and contemplative, he was prone to ponder the mysteries of life and the suffering of people he saw around him. Always sensing himself as being somehow connected to the "spirit world," as a young man that feeling was further heightened when for seven days he underwent an experience of extended perception in which it appeared to Jakob that his whole consciousness was awakening and expanding. Later, at the age of twenty-five, a second visionary experience caused Jakob to believe that the foundation of all that existed had been revealed to him. He became convinced that somehow he had gazed into the very mystery of Creation itself:

In one quarter of an hour I saw and knew more than if I had been many years together at a university, at which I did exceedingly admire, and I knew not how it happened to me; and therefore I turned my heart to praise God for it. For I saw and knew the Being of all beings, the Byss and Abyss, also the birth or eternal generation of the Holy Trinity; the descent and original of this world, and all creatures, through the divine wisdom.

Waite, et. al, 82

In time, Boehme would write more than thirty books about the nature of God and the information divulged to him during these and subsequent visionary experiences. Although branded a heretic by some of his contemporaries, his works would have a profound and lasting influence on later philosophers and religious leaders, including Emmanuel Swedenborg, William Blake, John Wesley and George Fox.

Apart from the occurrence of cosmic consciousness—in which a person's entire awareness seems to become transformed—history has recorded a variety of ways in which individuals have professed personal encounters with the Divine. Some of these encounters appear to be more transitory and do not necessarily embody as total and long lasting a change in awareness, although the experience is no less significant to the individual. One example is the experience of reportedly hearing the voice of God.

For thousands of years Jewish tradition has accepted the possibility of hearing God's voice and has labeled this type of encounter the *Bat Kol.* According to Rabbinical scholars, the voice of God has been known to communicate with individuals, groups, communities, rulers and even entire nations. Characteristics of this voice include a unique or remarkable sound as well as the invisibility of the speaker. (The Jewish Encyclopedia, 588) In some cases it is like the "still small voice" heard by the Old Testament prophet Elijah after he had journeyed into the wilderness to escape the wrath of Jezebel and was reportedly told by God to return to Damascus (I Kings 19:12). On other occasions it may be as loud as the sound of a trumpet, such as the voice heard by the Apostle John during his exile on the isle of Patmos while he was experiencing the Revelation (Revelation 1:10). In addition to the quality of the voice, both tradition and scripture assert that thunder, an earthquake, or a powerful bright light may accompany the experience.

The Old and New Testaments as well as the Jewish Talmud and Midrash detail literally dozens of examples of the Bat Kol. Apparently this voice is heard whenever the Divine Will needs to be communicated, whether to solitary individuals or to humankind in general. For example, Moses, the Old Testament lawgiver who delivered the Hebrew slaves out of Egypt, had repeated experiences with the Bat Kol (Exodus 3:4, Exodus 6:2, Exodus 9:1, and others) but perhaps none more momentous than when God chose to communicate the Ten Commandments (Exodus 20). New Testament examples include a Divine voice coming out of heaven to acknowledge Jesus during his baptism by John the Baptist (Matthew 3:17), as well as Saul's transformative experience on the road to Damascus when he was reproached for persecuting the Christian sect (Acts 9:3–4).

Besides people literally hearing the voice of God, the Bible reports numerous instances when the Divine Will has been communicated through dreams, including the announcement that "If there be a prophet among you, I the Lord will make myself known unto him in a vision, and will speak unto him in a dream." (Numbers 12:6) In fact, throughout history many cultures have believed that it is not uncommon for the Divine to speak to individuals through their dreams. As a case in point, the Greeks placed much importance on dreams and established temples dedicated to Asclepius, the god of healing, where individuals could come and receive dream guidance. At these temples individuals would ask for a dream, hoping that the gods would appear and prescribe a course of treatment for their illness.

Numerous religious traditions place significance on the ability of individuals to obtain Divine guidance or information in their dreams. According to legend, around 560 B.C., Queen Maya of Lumbini, Nepal, had a dream in which the most beautiful elephant she had ever seen entered her womb. In Hinduism, the elephant-headed god of wisdom and problem solving is Ganesh. Queen Maya described this elephant as perfect in appearance and with a radiance that was "more brilliant than the moon or the sun." (DeBecker, 42) After hearing her dream, Hindu Brahmin told the queen the interpretation of the dream was that she was destined to give birth to a universal monarch. The dream proved prophetic, for Maya eventually gave birth to a son, Prince Siddhartha, who gave up his royal birthright and became the Buddha.

Dreams also played a role in the establishment of Islam in the sixth century. According to legend, during his merchant travels Mohammed became distressed that God's revelations through various prophets like Abraham, Moses, and Jesus had become subject to idolatry and superstition. Deeply troubled by the way in which the word of God had become corrupted, Mohammed sought solace in a desert cave. By some accounts he spent six months in prayer, fasting and meditation and had frequent dreams that dealt with the thoughts of his waking mind. During one of these dreams Mohammed was awakened by the voice of the angel Gabriel who presented a cloth covered with writing for Mohammed to read. In spite of Mohammed's confession that he was illiterate and unable to read, divine intervention made it possible and the prophet "instantly felt his understanding illumined with celestial light, and read what was written on the cloth, which contained the decrees of God, as afterwards promulgated in the Koran." (Irving, 37) The prophet also used dreams to establish the frequency and method by which the faithful were to be called to daily prayer.

Approximately one hundred years after the archangel Gabriel's first appearance to Mohammed, another archangel would make several attempts to communicate information from the realm of spirit to the mortal world of humankind. According to the legend, in the year 708 the archangel Michael appeared in a dream to Aubert, bishop of Avranches, France. The archangel instructed the bishop to build a chapel on top of Mont Tombe, one mile off the coast of Normandy. The absurdity of the request caused the bishop to ignore the command. It occurred a second time, and still the bishop did nothing to follow through on the dream. Finally, the archangel Michael appeared in person and struck the bishop with a blazing angelic finger, reportedly leaving a permanent indentation in Aubert's skull. The bishop needed no further encouragement to begin his task, and finally the chapel that would become Mont Saint Michel five hundred years later was begun. The Bible also provides numerous accounts of angelic messengers conveying Divine Will or judgment.

The story of an angelic encounter laying the groundwork for the establishment of a powerful religious movement occurred in the United States during the nineteenth century to Joseph Smith (1805–1844) of upstate New York. Smith testified that he had experienced a series of visions beginning in 1823 that encouraged him to restore true Christianity to God's kingdom on earth. In time, an angel named Moroni would reveal to Smith a set of golden plates that were written in an undecipherable form of hieroglyphics. The angel also provided Smith with a set of "seer stones"—the Biblical equivalent of the Urim and

Thummim—that were to be used for translating the plates. Beginning in 1827, Joseph Smith translated the ancient plates shown to him by Moroni, eventually resulting in the publication of the *Book of Mormon* in 1830.

On the other side of the world, a variety of visionary encounters occurred in the life of Paramahansa Yogananda (1893–1952), founder of the Self-Realization Fellowship and author of the classic *Autobiography of a Yogi.* Born to an upper-class family in India, he spent his early years becoming acquainted with many of India's spiritual masters while on his own journey of personal enlightenment. At the age of twenty-two he took the vows of a Hindu monk and spent much of the rest of his life traveling around the world speaking to ecumenical audiences about the underlying unity of the world's religions and the reality of direct experiences with the Divine.

One of Yogananda's most memorable encounters occurred in 1936 while on a lecture engagement in Bombay. At the time, he was looking through his third-story hotel window and witnessed a vision of Lord Krishna in shimmering brilliance floating above the rooftop of a building across the street. Completely uplifted, the yogi accepted the vision as a premonition of some great spiritual event. One week later, Yogananda would have an extraordinary two-hour encounter with his guru, Sri Yukteswar, who had been dead for three months! (Yogananda, 399)

Outside of scripture, legend and religious history, one of the most prominent contemporary examples of encountering the Divine came in the form of Dr. Raymond A. Moody, Jr.'s international best-seller, *Life After Life*, in 1975. Dr. Moody brought to public awareness the phenomena of the *Near Death Experience* in which individuals clinically "die" only to be later revived and able to relate their death experience. Regardless of an individual's background, the Near Death Experience seems to contain various similarities among recipients, such as a life review, a reluctance to leave the spiritual realm, and an encounter with a Being of Light. According to Moody's research, the description of this Being has many common elements and is not affected by the individual's religious background:

> Typically, at its first appearance this light is dim, but it rapidly gets brighter until it reaches an unearthly brilliance. Yet, even though this light (usually said to be white or "clear") is of an indescribable brilliance, many make the specific point that it does not in any way hurt their eyes or dazzle them, or keep them from seeing other things around them . . .
>
> Despite the light's unusual manifestation, however, not one person has expressed any doubt whatsoever that it was a being, a being of light. Not only that, it is a personal being. It has a very definite personality. The love and the warmth which emanate from this being to the dying person are utterly beyond words, and he [or she] feels completely surrounded by it and taken up in it, completely at ease and accepted in the presence of this being.
>
> Moody, 58–59

Identified by some as Christ, others God, and still others an angel, the Being accompanies a life review and generally communicates the fact that it is not time for the individual to die. Afterwards, the "deceased" individual reluctantly returns to her or his body and is revived from the death experience.

Experiences such as these and others suggest that encounters with the Divine have occurred in a variety of ways throughout the history of humankind: experiences in cosmic consciousness, hearing the voice of God, dreams, visions, angelic apparitions, and the Near Death Experience. Regardless of their different manifestations, individuals who attest to a personal encounter with the Divine generally claim that the experience suddenly filled them with a sense of mental elation or a joyous wonderment. Many report that there is often an accompanying feeling of hope and encouragement—giving the individual the sense that he or she is not alone in facing the challenges of life. There can also be a renewed sense of empowerment, causing the recipient to believe that she or he has the ability and the determination to continue on. Sometimes individuals may question why their Divine encounter was bestowed upon them in the first place; however, in spite of this questioning, generally their faith and their own sense of self are strengthened because of the experience. Oftentimes these encounters lead to a fresh appreciation for life and a new reverence for individuals from every religious background and level of society. For some the experience is so unforgettable that its memory will last a lifetime; for others the encounter has the effect of literally changing an entire lifetime.

In describing cosmic consciousness, Richard Bucke alluded to the impact his own personal experience would have upon the rest of his life. Discussing his account in the third person, Dr. Bucke expressed its significance as follows:

> Among other things he did not come to believe, he saw and knew that the Cosmos is not dead matter but a living Presence, that the soul of man is immortal, that the universe is so built and ordered that without any peradventure all things work together for the good of each and all, that the foundation principle of the world is what we call love and that the happiness of every one is in the long run absolutely certain. He claims that he learned more within the few seconds during which the illumination lasted than in previous months or even years of study, and that he learned much that no study could ever have taught.
>
> The illumination itself continued not more than a few moments, but its effects proved ineffaceable; it was impossible for him ever to forget what he at that time saw and knew; neither did he, or could he, ever doubt the truth of what was then presented to his mind.
>
> Bucke, 10

According to their own accounts, individuals who have had an experience with the Divine have been positively affected in many different ways. Those in the midst of loss were comforted. Those who were confused became enlightened. Those who touched death no longer feared it. Those who were ill or broken were somehow healed. Those who had lost their faith found it. Those who were overwhelmed by the cares of life, no matter how large or small, felt the helpful presence of something much greater, making it clear that even in the grand scheme of an infinite universe, they still mattered. With these things in mind, this book is written with the hope that it might provide some illumination to the question of whether or not something beyond the physical world actually maintains an ongoing concern for all of humankind. It also attempts to find similarities between these Divine encounters—what kind of commonality they engender among those who have them. Finally, it explores the premise that there may be much more to us than a physical body.

1

Personal Encounters with the Divine

> **And the earth have We spread out, and have flung firm hills therein, and have caused of every lovely kind to grow thereon . . . We verily created man and We know what his soul whispereth to him, and We are nearer to him than his jugular vein.**
>
> **The Koran**
> **QAF: 50.07 & 50.16**

Starr Daily was a confirmed criminal. At the age of twelve he began drinking. Liquor led to a life of stealing. From the time of his early teens he had moved from one crime to another. His antisocial behavior and his criminal record—including a stint as a safecracker for Al Capone—would result in many years behind bars. As a youth, he saw the activities of well-meaning social workers hoping to reform him only as a way to affect a pardon or a commuted sentence rather than as a means for true transformation of character. He became adept at telling lies and making idle promises—trading his dishonesty for immunity as often as he could get away with it. He considered crime an expression of his true self. In spite of many attempts by others to reform him, a variety of persuasive individuals and threats, repeated incarceration, and even torture, Daily remained a convict, both in action and in state of mind.

However, one day something happened that would completely transform him. According to Starr Daily, "In one moment I was a criminal. In the next I was healed." (Daily, *Release*, xi) By the 1940s, he was a reformed individual with an incredible depth of love for all humankind, a published author several times over, and a much sought-after speaker. He was an advocate for prison reform, a spokesperson for religious ministries, and a frequently cited example of the power of spiritual transformation. While in prison, a personal encounter with the Divine had changed his life forever.

Long before Daily's metamorphosis, a number of youthful experiences had apparently laid the foundation for his criminal misdeeds. According to friends, several childhood incidents had been responsible for creating a deep-seated fear—a fear which Daily cited as being at the heart of his life of crime. To begin with, his mother had died after his birth. Her death was followed by a couple of experiences as a schoolboy that Daily would remember for the rest of his life.

On one occasion, Starr Daily had been mercilessly belittled in front of an entire class for forgetting his words during a public presentation—an incident that would cause him to be terrified of public speaking. Another event occurred when he was about eleven or twelve. At the time his stepmother took him to a Pentecostal revival. Throughout the revival, the minister preached a horrifying sermon about the fires of hell and the immeasurable influence of Satan. From that time on, Daily lived in fear, and his attempts to overcome that fear by proving how tough he was became the root cause of his criminal behavior.

After these childhood events, he couldn't help but feel different from other kids—as though he had been born with some sort of a quirk that made him a criminal. By his own admission, he did not feel responsible for his actions. His crime spree would eventually lead to his first period of incarceration as an adult. After his release from prison, he managed to acquire a job in a shoe factory. While behind bars he had become quite adept at making garments with a sewing machine—a background that obviously came in handy for the factory position. However, knowing that the company would never hire a former convict on parole, Daily was forced to lie about his background.

Surprisingly, he liked his job in the factory and had almost decided that turning straight and earning an honest living might be possible. Unfortunately, one day on his way to work he was spotted by the very detective who had been responsible for his incarceration. The detective apparently felt obligated to inform the employer about Daily's true background, resulting in the shoe factory firing him on the spot. Throwing aside his resolution to become an honest citizen, Daily says he became even more bitter and "walked away from that job with a poisoned heart and a bitter resolution eating into my brain like a cancer." From that time on, his approach to life might best be expressed as intolerance for all other people.

He spent years as an outcast, even behind bars. He was known for his anger, his antagonism toward authority, and his self-serving approach to life. His early fears had caused him to become so callous that he came across as being without fear. Because he was so filled with antagonism and prone to antisocial behaviors, in prison he often found himself in solitary confinement. Other prisoners knew he was not to be messed with—he resisted interrogation and refused to break even under torture. For fourteen years he was a recurring inmate. Still, prison life was not easy for him. On one occasion, Daily recalled one of his own torturous experiences while behind bars:

> For two days and nights I had been subjected to "third degree" police methods in an effort to torture a confession out of me. My head had been beaten with a rubber hose until it resembled a huge stone bruise, swollen beyond human shape, my face black from the congealed blood beneath the surface. Lighted cigars had been pressed against my flesh. I had hung for three hours with my wrists handcuffed over a hot steam pipe. My arms had been twisted behind me and my elbows beaten with blackjacks until the bones felt crunchy. Heavy heels had ground my bare feet against a concrete floor. On the third night of this I was about at the end of my endurance. Daily, Prison, 5

According to Daily, his Divine encounter came after an experience of being punished in "the dungeon," a place where prisoners were chained with each wrist elevated above their heads and hung for up to twelve-hour stretches for a maximum of fifteen days. The hanging caused a prisoner's legs and arms to swell and his feet to turn black from congealed blood. The heart became weakened from the strain, necessitating a doctor's presence and regular check-ups to make certain that the prisoner's body could continue to withstand the punishment.

During one of his extended confinements in the dungeon cell, he began to fade in and out of consciousness. The stress on his body became so severe that his mind no longer seemed to be his own. When he had reached the point where he doubted his ability to survive, he began having a series of senseless dreams—dreams apparently without beginning or end. Suddenly, he had a memorable dream about Jesus, a man, Daily confessed, whom he had spent years "trying to hate":

> The whole picture had that quiet clarity about it that draws out thematic details of expression, of feeling, of thought, of purpose. He came toward me, his lips moving as though in prayer. He stopped near me eventually and stood looking down. I had never seen such love in human eye; I had never felt so utterly enveloped in love. I seemed to know consciously that I had seen and felt something that would influence my life throughout all eternity.
> Daily, Prison, 36

After he had felt the power of this intense love, Daily next became aware of each of the individuals he had somehow injured throughout his life of crime. One by one he felt prompted to send each one of them the same love he had just encountered. When he had finished the experience of sending love to those he had harmed, he suddenly began to visualize all of the people in life whom he had felt injured by. In the same way, he sent them love, as well. At the end of his experience, Daily knew that something momentous had happened and that his personal consciousness as well as his approach to life had been changed forever:

> I knew that I had transcended all personal and bodily limitations of habit and environment which had bound me through the years. I had no sense of my prison walls, but my thoughts roamed the imponderable Universe far and clear. The measurements of Time and Space vanished out of my consciousness. I was free. I knew I was free. I had found the Reality within the actuality, the breath within the breath, the consciousness within the consciousness, the soul within the form. And above all, I knew that I was being what theologians call reborn. Daily, Release, 47

After the experience and with the help and advice of a fellow convict named Dad Trueblood, Daily learned about the incredible power of love—even while behind bars. He learned how to get along with even the most angry and antisocial of criminals. He realized that he wanted to live because he finally had something to live for. Because of his change in character, Daily was eventually elevated to the position of night nurse in the prison hospital—a position that enabled him to be of service to those who suffered a variety of physical, mental and spiritual ills. His work became a small contribution towards making amends for all of his former offenses against society. To be sure, his spiritual transformation was surprising even to him because throughout the years, many prison chaplains had tried to give him religion but to no avail.

Because of his depth of transformation, he was eventually paroled from prison in March 1930. Not long after his release, he began a very effective prison ministry. Repeatedly, he was asked to go into prisons to tell his story. He wrote articles and became quite professional at public speaking—overcoming one of his childhood fears in the process. His first book, *Love Can Open Prison Doors,* was published in 1934. After its publication, he received hundreds of letters from around the world, including from evangelist Glenn Clark, who was attempting to establish retreat-like camps throughout the country where individuals could come together and find their own balance: spiritually, mentally, and physically. Extremely impressed with Starr Daily's story and his ability to inspire others, Clark made Daily a permanent speaker at his CFO (Camp Farthest Out) programs. When discussing Daily's amazing transformation, Clark once wrote:

> Starr is, himself, the greatest of all miracles. He is the walking evidence that the miracle that happened once to Saul of Tarsus on the Damascus road could happen again and again. For an even greater one happened to him. When a man had been a thoroughly conditioned criminal for a quarter of a century, pronounced incorrigible by psychiatrists and judges, and then in one night is completely changed and dedicated to Christ, all other miracles fade into significance before it. Clark, et. al, 1

In time, Starr Daily married and continued his prison ministry, his speaking engagements, and his writing. In all, he would be responsible for countless presentations, numerous articles and more than a dozen publications. For the next thirty years and throughout the rest of his life, he held audiences and individuals spellbound by his lectures, and his life proved to be a true testimonial to the power of love. By all accounts, until his death in the 1970s, Starr Daily had become an inspiration to thousands because of a personal encounter with the Divine that had changed his life forever.

■

Although she never experienced a literal prison, in many respects life for Milly Peters[1] was like being in prison. Born as the only girl into a family of three children, her older brother was mentally retarded and a constant challenge to his family. Her father was a World War II airborne veteran, but the trauma of war had placed him in an institution for battle fatigue, and according to family members he was never the same afterwards. Prone to be argumentative and easily angered, he had a hard time holding down a job because of his propensity to fight. At home he was cruel and physically abusive. Milly was no better off with her mother, for the woman was not interested in being a parent and even blamed her youngest son's birth for nearly killing her during the pregnancy. Whenever her mother grew tired of parenting, Milly and her younger brother were simply placed in the care of their mentally handicapped sibling.

Criticized constantly for her behavior, her actions, and even her appearance, Milly did not feel as though she belonged anywhere. At school she was painfully shy and was subjected to constant taunting because of the stigma of having a mentally retarded brother. As a child she was sickly and anemic and had scoliosis of the lower spine, causing her to spend a lot of time in physical therapy. She was terrified of the dark and had frequent night terrors. Her childhood home was filthy—filled with ashtrays, dirt, and countless fleas from the attack dogs that her father

---

[1]For the most part, other than historical or published accounts that are cited, the names used within this volume have been changed to maintain confidentiality.

insisted on keeping in the house for his own protection. Most of their once-a-week baths were given from the sink because the bathtub was filled with feces due to her elder brother's mental condition and the fact that he had frequent intestinal problems. Sometimes her father would come home at 2 a.m. and choose to discipline his eldest son for what the boy had done in the tub, awakening everyone in the household:

He would come home and fill the tub with scalding hot water and throw my brother in it as punishment for his defect. My youngest brother and I would lie in our beds and sweat until the screaming stopped. And then we'd have to get up to go to school. Sometimes there was water that had run down the hallway just outside our doors. And we would get it on our shoes and end up smelling horrible ourselves. The best way I could figure out what to do was to be as perfect as possible.

But no matter how hard Milly tried, she was never good enough for her parents. Her parents often whipped her, and the threat of God was used as a tool for discipline. She was told that she would burn in hell forever because of her behavior. Although she became mad at God for giving her such a life, she constantly prayed and asked for forgiveness for whatever she might have done. Milly Peters was only eleven years old.

When her oldest brother's behavior became impossible to control, he was made a ward of the state and institutionalized. Her parents eventually divorced, and Milly managed to get herself married and out of the house at sixteen. Unfortunately, her husband was nearly as abusive as her father had been, and the marriage lasted only six years, during which time she had one son.

Eventually, Milly would remarry, have a much better situation, and have two more children. However, the feelings of worthlessness, the self-criticism, and the suppressed anger remained with her. She felt as though she could not do anything right and had failed miserably at her life. She was afraid to work. She was afraid to drive. She was afraid of failure. But at the age of thirty-six, she felt an urgency to be doing something different. For months she wondered about where she was supposed to be and what she was supposed to be doing. She constantly prayed for guidance and frequently spoke about her concerns with her husband. One night as she brought the subject up "for the millionth time," her husband finally got up and went to the phone, looked through the phone book, and dialed a number to a Baptist church, even though they were Methodists at the time. The pastor was in his office preparing his sermon for the following morning, and Milly's husband simply handed her the phone:

"Tell him what you've been telling me."

She explained what she had been feeling, and the pastor promised to come over to her house on the following Tuesday evening. He ended the conversation by suggesting that she "expect a miracle," a statement that Milly thought strange at the time. But she was willing to do anything that might help solve her dilemma. When Tuesday arrived, the pastor came to the house as promised, bringing an associate pastor with him. According to Milly, they had a wonderful discussion and talked about many things: "my life, my family, my goals in life." And then the pastor invited the three of them to join together in prayer:

He wanted me to repeat a prayer after him. I knew I would probably mess this beautiful moment up. That was the thought that ran through my mind. But I would give it a try. After all, what was one more screw up in a million? We began. We were doing really well until I realized that I hadn't heard the last few words he had spoken in the prayer. So as to not totally ruin the moment, I said, "I didn't hear you." He didn't hear me, and it was then I realized that he was wearing a hearing aid. So as not to yell, I reached over and grabbed his hand. The other fellow took my other hand. He then went on . . . All at once, we began to tremble. I did not open my eyes but for a moment or two I had the brief thought that I had gotten mixed up with a weird cult or something—how typical of me.

Suddenly, Milly felt as though someone had turned on a sprinkler of water and placed it on the floor at her feet. The water was warm and rose up her body. Her hands began to feel on fire—a sensation that would last four days. The warmth rose through her body. The sensation persisted as though something were cleansing her entire being. When it finally subsided, Milly realized that something truly wonderful had just happened to her:

> My childhood nightmares and bad dreams were gone! I wasn't afraid of the dark anymore. The world I had lived in all my life was suddenly bright and beautiful. I felt confidence. I felt like I could do things I had never done before: drive a car and not be afraid, get a job and not be afraid of failure.

When she told the pastor what had happened, he only laughed and said, "I told you to expect a miracle." The transformation became permanent, and Milly was no longer the same. She became a new person that day and is convinced that her experience was "a miracle." Since then her life has changed immensely:

> I realize that my life has been a series of long and hard lessons, but I have learned compassion even when there was none for me. I have learned to love in spite of the not-so-loving person or persons in front of me. I have learned to forgive . . . I also have learned not to give up and die like I wanted to so many times before. I have become strong. I have learned that beyond the smiles on other peoples' faces, there is pain in us all. And I have learned to be kind to all of my fellow wounded souls.

In summing up her experience, Milly says, "When I love, I get the greatest satisfaction inside of myself—where I once thought I couldn't feel anything. It doesn't matter how everyone else loves me because God loves me. In fact, He likes me and I love and like Him too."

■

The case of Gladys Newsome was evidence of the Near Death Experience long before it was popularized in the 1970s. Now in her eighties, Gladys can still recall the experience as though it were yesterday, even though more than sixty years have passed. At the time, she was twenty-one, pregnant, and so poor that she and her husband "didn't have enough money for me to go to the hospital for the birthing and we didn't have enough money for a doctor to come to the house." To make matters worse, her husband had been in an accident and was laid up with a broken sternum. Gladys recalls:

He was out of work and we couldn't scrape together any money for ourselves, let alone what we needed for a doctor. Back then it was only thirty-five dollars to have a baby at the hospital—and that included the doctor's fee and being put up at the hospital for ten days to two weeks . . . thirty-five dollars and we didn't have it!

The couple had each been raised as Mormon and thankfully had a few family members who could provide a little assistance. Because they could not afford a doctor, Gladys' mother-in-law (a part-time midwife) came to help with the birth. It was Gladys' first child, and she really hadn't known what to expect. However, the birth pains became so severe that it became clear that Gladys was having a problem.

The labor pains persisted for many hours. A whole day passed. Well into the night Gladys' pains continued without relenting until all she could do was scream out in pain. Although the severity of the pains lessened on occasion, their intensity persisted until Gladys began to believe that the pain was more than she could bear. With each passing hour, Gladys felt herself becoming weaker: "I was in labor so long and in so much pain, that I felt myself start to fade." Finally, just as her baby was about to be born, Gladys felt herself beginning to leave her body.

She became cognizant of the fact that she was dying. All at once the pain seemed to stop, and she became aware of the most vibrant blue color she had ever seen. The colors intensified until her vision was filled with pale blue and gold, and suddenly Gladys saw the most beautiful staircase:

I started going up those stairs, feeling very much at peace. The stairs were small and easy to walk up—I almost felt like I was gliding. Suddenly, I saw that there were all kinds of people on the stairs around me, and I felt very much at peace and comforted. I forgot all about the pain or even having a baby. I was just taken up by the beauty of the scene around me.

Meanwhile, the midwife felt Gladys' body go limp. All at once, from somewhere in the back of her mind, Gladys heard her mother-in-law scream out, "Honey, you can't do this to us! There's a little baby trying to come into the world! Don't do this to us!"

Immediately, Gladys was stopped in her movement up the stairs. She felt a severe pain in her head, and suddenly she became conscious of being pulled back into her body. The beauty of the staircase disappeared from her sight, and she heard the cries of an infant. Gladys had given birth to a son.

Since her experience occurred long before the notoriety of the Near Death Experience, Gladys kept it to herself and told very few individuals. However, the trauma of the birthing caused her to stay in bed for two weeks. The difficulties of her pregnancy remained evident even two weeks later when she finally got out of bed only to faint a short time later from exhaustion.

Today, Gladys is an elderly woman with two children, both in their sixties. She has six grandchildren and seven great-grandchildren. She also has no fears of death or of what might happen to her when she dies, for according to Gladys, "I saw Heaven that day and I have no doubt that I will see it again."

■

The story of Michael Franks is one that is evidence of the possibility of several different encounters occurring in one individual's life. Born in Brooklyn to Jewish parents, Michael often felt as though he didn't belong in his own family. His grandparents and parents were orthodox and very conservative, whereas his beliefs and perspective were often much more open and expansive. Because his outlook on life was vastly different from theirs, he frequently felt chastised and alienated. Because he was sensitive and desperately needed their love and acceptance, he often felt broken-hearted, especially when they chastised him, put him down, or asked "What's wrong with you?" when his views differed from their own. As a result, he often had problems with his father and his brother.

When Michael was thirteen years old, he found his life's work after being exposed to Latin music. From that time on, he knew that he wanted music to be his life's direction—a decision that his parents repeatedly fought. As a means of financing his love for music, he became a carpenter by trade. Even today, he considers himself a drummer first and a carpenter second.

Eventually, he met a woman he loved. They became engaged and moved into an apartment together. He felt his life was going along just fine: he had a fiancée, a good job, and his music, and he was looking forward to his future. However, it was not long before his entire life seemed to fall apart. He lost his job. A close relative died. Both of his parents became hospitalized. Worst of all, his fiancée ended their engagement "and kicked me out of her life and our apartment." His life had suddenly and dramatically changed.

All of this occurred within a period of three months, causing Michael to feel that he was on the edge of an abyss, barely hanging on with his fingernails: "The emotional pain was devastating. At one point the pain was so great I just wanted to stop, anyway I could, if you know what I mean. At night, I cried myself to sleep." As a means of coping, Michael used marijuana and snorted cocaine. To make matters worse, during his depression Michael began having a recurring dream of being chased by a lion. The lion was vicious and meant to destroy him. Repeatedly, he awoke terrified and found that he was wearing sweat-drenched pajamas. Although he tried to survive this period as best as he could, Michael credits three experiences as being responsible for turning his life around: a visionary presence, his work with a therapist, and his meeting an elderly Jewish woman named Mrs. Steinberg.

The vision occurred the day after a particularly intense "lion dream," while Michael was on his way home from a job. Because he had been out of work, Michael had been forced to go into contracting for himself. During the drive home, he was thinking about the dream and how it had terrified him the night before. All at once, he felt a warm feeling growing inside of his chest. The warmth became so intense that all thoughts of the dream were pushed from his mind; the warmth began to spread from his chest to his entire body:

I was enveloped in a warmth and a glow that I have never felt before. Suddenly, as this warmth spread out to my arms and limbs, I could see rays of golden light shooting out of my arms and hands. I just kept breathing, trying not to think but just to feel. I was in such joy and peace that words are hard to describe it accurately.

As I looked out onto the highway before me, the colors of the world became rich and vibrant. The greens of the grasses and trees on the side of the road jumped out at me, almost as if the colors themselves were alive. The blue of the sky was breathtaking. Even the black of the asphalt road was the deepest black I had ever seen. At that point my van seemed to lift off the road and hover just a few inches off the ground. I was still moving down the road at a good speed, but I could swear I wasn't on the road.

There I was with the van seemingly suspended in space, the vibrant colors of the world flooding my senses, the golden light shooting out of my arms and hands, and this incredible warmth and peace inside me.

It seemed like a long time but actually lasted only about ninety seconds. But I shall never forget that moment in my life—a glimpse into the Divine.

Shortly thereafter, Michael began seeing a therapist who specialized in guided imagery. With her assistance he was able to go deep inside himself and pull out all of the anger and traumatic experiences that had occurred in his life. It wasn't an easy process for him; he went through a great deal of crying, "not just a few drops of tears, I mean deep abdominal sobbing." He began to uncover many childhood traumas that he had blocked from his conscious mind. In time, he would recognize them as the angry lion that had been chasing him.

While he was still in therapy, one of his first jobs as an independent contractor was to take care of several repairs on a big house owned by a Mr. and Mrs. Steinberg, who lived about twenty minutes away. Still in a great deal of emotional pain, Michael woke up each morning crying. However, every morning when he arrived for work, Mrs. Steinberg made him coffee and biscuits and would not let him work until they had chatted. Her husband was at work, and her children had grown, and she wanted to talk to someone. It wasn't too long before Michael and

Mrs. Steinberg began sharing their feelings. Even now, Michael calls her "a god-send."

He kept her company, and she sympathized with his problems. She often spoke about her childhood home in Jerusalem. Their relationship grew, and they became good friends. She helped him process his feelings, and he prevented her from feeling lonely. When he finished one job in the house, she would think of another one. Finally, the work on the Steinberg house came to an end, and Michael moved on to other jobs, but the two kept in touch. As the months passed, Mrs. Steinberg gave him a few more things to do on her house, and they often communicated by phone.

Therapy helped Michael overcome his self-doubt. He overcame the anger he had felt toward his family. He was able to release his emotions and begin to affirm his own self-worth. His dreams about the lion lessened, and when he did have them, he was able to turn and face the lion head-on. Eventually the dreams ceased altogether. When he was well on the road to recovery, he had a memorable dream about Mrs. Steinberg. Several months had passed since they had last spoken:

In the dream, a young, good-looking woman appeared to me. Although I knew Mrs. Steinberg only as an elderly woman, I knew this young woman was Mrs. Steinberg. She was standing outside on a landscape that I didn't recognize . . . Her face was young and fresh. She had a "glow" to her, as if her entire body had a light behind her and all you could see was the luminosity of her silhouette.

She started talking to me, but I don't remember the exact words. I do remember the tone of her words. They were supportive, affectionate, and uplifting. If was as if she was cheering me on. I felt really good.

Michael awoke and wrote the dream down. A few days passed, and he decided to call Mrs. Steinberg just to say hello and to share the dream with her. When he called, Mrs. Steinberg's husband answered the phone and told Michael that she had died two weeks earlier of stomach cancer. Mr. Steinberg added that she had been buried in Jerusalem, her childhood home. Michael hung up the phone saddened, for having lost a dear friend. At the same time, however, he felt convinced that in his dream he had seen Mrs. Steinberg in the Jerusalem desert, just as she had appeared as a young girl. He felt blessed that she had come to him.

Today Michael realizes that although the day his fiancée kicked him out of the house was one of the saddest and most painful events in his life, it was really a blessing in disguise. If it had not been for his ex-girlfriend, he would never have felt the pain that led to his therapy, his visionary experience, or even his closeness to Mrs. Steinberg. He no longer drinks or does drugs. His business is booming, and his musical career is taking off. He has healed the rift between himself and his father and has begun to heal the broken relationship with his brother. He feels that divine intervention transformed his life and since then his spirit has "soared":

> I have never felt so in touch with myself, the natural world or the rest of humanity. My life is blessed with peace of mind, a pure heart, good health and more money than I ever had before. I am in a good space, ready for whatever comes my way.
>
> My ancestry is Jewish but I love the teachings of Jesus. My brother-in-law practices Tibetan Buddhism. I feel that they are all saying the same thing with different accents . . .
>
> My spiritual experiences range from the profound calm of Zen to the beautiful and powerful ceremonial drums of West Africa. I have been Bar Mitzvahed, and I have taken Holy Communion. I have done sweat lodges with Native Americans in Montana, and I have worshipped African deities in the Bronx. I see and experience truth and beauty in all the varieties of religious expression.

■

In the case of Joanie Wyatt, she was a twenty-eight-year-old student going to chiropractic school, when a "supernatural" experience convinced her of the possibility of Divine intervention in everyday life. At the time of her experience, Joanie felt overwhelmed with a variety of financial and emotional stresses. Supporting herself by working while taking thirty credits each semester proved to be overwhelming: "my mental stress was extreme and very consuming, often making studying all that much harder." To make matters worse, Joanie suffered from low self-esteem and often wondered whether or not she had the ability or even the destiny to follow through on her dream.

One day, as a means of relaxing and just getting away from the pressures while getting some exercise, Joanie decided to take a bike ride by herself. Unfortunately, the road was well traveled and frequently intersected by cross roads that often appeared just over the hill—making them difficult to see, according to Joanie, "until you are right on top of them." She was pedaling quite fast, keeping up a good momentum, and all at once she saw a car enter the cross street at the same moment she did:

> Neither one of us saw the other until the second we were about to collide. We were so close that I could see him brace himself (as did I) because we were both moving too fast to avoid the collision. In that moment I felt a strange weightlessness and timelessness. It was a sensation that is hard to describe—it was like a time warp. In bracing myself for the impact, I had shut my eyes. When I finally opened them, I found that I was safe and well past the car. I turned and saw the driver sitting there with his mouth opened, equally stunned.

According to Joanie, the only explanation is that something had intervened and saved her from an accident:

> There was absolutely no possible way we wouldn't collide! I can still remember the feeling of somehow being lifted and briefly taken out of time. As I recall, it seems like there was also an absence of all sound. The moment also seemed longer than it could have been. I didn't see anything, but I know that I experienced Divine intervention. I would have been killed or seriously injured.

Today, Joanie owns her own chiropractic practice. She has also managed to move beyond her thoughts of worthlessness, in part because of the accident that did not occur: "It made me realize that perhaps I had value, that I was being watched over and perhaps my life had a destiny after all." Since the experience, her spiritual belief system has evolved dramatically, to the point where she is convinced that "there are as many paths to God as there are people." With that in mind, she has become a student of comparative religions, exploring Christianity, Buddhism the Hopi religion, as well as the "practice of coming to know God through nature."

■

In another contemporary experience, Margie Greggs believes that she also encountered Divine intervention in her own life for several reasons. First of all, the experience confirmed her belief in the existence of the Divine, even though she had been angry with God at the time. It also made it possible for her to leave a dangerous situation with her husband because she really had not been strong enough to leave on her own. Finally, she believes it enabled her to live and pursue the life that was truly supposed to be a part of her soul's destiny.

For six years Margie had been married to an alcoholic named Art who was known for his drinking binges. In addition to alcohol, her husband also had a problem believing in any God—leading to many arguments between husband and wife. To make matters worse, Art was not in control of himself when he drank, and he drank often.

In spite of their marriage problems, Margie did not feel strong enough to leave the situation. In fact, the couple was getting ready to move from Texas to North Carolina in order to be closer to family members. Two nights before the planned move, Margie and Art were out late having pizza for dinner. Her husband had also been on a two-week drinking binge and was drunk. Margie had sipped two glasses of beer through dinner.

Because of her husband's intoxication, Margie drove the car home. It spite of the fact that the car was in fine mechanical shape and had never had any problems before, it cut off three times on the way, causing her to wonder what was happening. When they finally got home, Margie helped Art into the bedroom only to have him pass out on top of her. She got out from under him, left him asleep on the bed, and went out to the living room sofa. It was about 2 a.m., and she was simply sitting there thinking about her life situation and how she was going to get everything ready for the move. According to Margie, all at once something happened:

Suddenly, a voice spoke to me saying, "Get out of there!" I didn't know what to think, and I hesitated maybe one or two minutes. Again, the same voice said, "Get out of there NOW!" At the very same moment, the right rabbit ear of the TV antenna began vibrating like crazy, pointing in the direction of the front door!

Margie decided she needed to head the advice. She ran into the bedroom to awaken her husband. It was quite a struggle but he finally came to—although he was not at all happy about being disturbed. She got him out of the house and the two of them walked to the bus station a couple of blocks away. Once they arrived, the night air had apparently instilled enough sobriety in Art that he was able to make a phone call while Margie sat waiting in the bus station. A short time later Margie was shocked to find that Art had called the police and was having her arrested for public drunkenness! She was taken to the police station where she called her parents. Her father promised to come get her even though the drive was many hours in duration.

A few hours later, one of the policemen came to the cell and told Margie that her husband was there and wanted to pay her bail. Margie refused. A short time later, the policeman asked once again, and still Margie refused. After the second refusal, Art returned to their home. When her father finally arrived, Margie was released. Rather than returning home, she rode with her father to her parents' house. Shortly after their arrival, there was a phone call, and Margie learned that there had been a fire at her home. That very night, their home had been destroyed and Art had been pronounced dead at the scene. Margie is convinced that had she not left the house as instructed, her husband would have eventually destroyed her one way or another.

Since that experience Margie has become very involved in both spiritual and physical healing. She has become a Reiki master and also works in one of the finest treatment centers for addiction in the country. She calls her Divine encounter a "life-saving experience," one that enabled her to get on with the rest of her life. She has also become convinced that even during the darkest moments of her life when it appeared that she was standing alone, "you are never really alone." She still finds it amazing that on the night of the tragedy, she was placed in jail—a place that was perhaps the safest in the entire city.

■

Another woman, Deborah Bradley, is convinced that one of her dreams proved to be "nothing short of Divine assistance," enabling her to move past years of judgment, anger and resentment. A single mother with two daughters from two different relationships, for various reasons Deborah remained angry with each of the girls' fathers, Peter and Steven, even though one of her children was a teenager and the other was twenty-four.

At a period in her life when Deborah became more interested in spiritual growth, she went to a Catholic retreat for personal renewal. After an evening presentation, she prayed for a personal message. That night she had a dream:

> I dreamt about Peter and Steven (the fathers of my two daughters). There was only one physical body, but the individual kept changing first from Peter, then to Steven. The individual who changed back and forth was sitting on the couch . . .
>
> [In the dream] I knew that Peter/Steven had cancer and was very unhappy, difficult and very unpleasant. I didn't want to get close to them. But we all went out to a jewelry store, saw a carousel (as big as a big building) and finally ended up in the apartment again.
>
> I could smell the rotting flesh from cancer. It was eating Peter/Steven, but no one talked about it. It kept me away from Peter/Steven.
>
> I knew that I should give Peter/Steven a hug because it was the right thing to do. The second I made that decision, I moved toward the couch where he was sitting. All at once the cancer was gone, and he appeared to be clean and smiling. I realized that one of my daughters was watching when I went to give him a hug. This was a true friendship kind of hug. The dream ended.

When Deborah awoke, she sensed that the cancer was the resentment and anger that she had held too long within herself against both men. She decided to write Peter and Steven each a letter. In the letters she thanked them for all the positive things they had been in her life and for their continued influence in her daughters' lives. She prayed and then mailed the letters.

The result was immediate and long lasting. According to Deborah, "I have been released from anger and I no longer carry the old baggage of grudges. I have more understanding, love, patience, and tolerance. I feel that the dream and the actions I took finally released me." Since that time, Deborah has continued to work on herself, her relationships and her desire to grow spiritually.

■

In another case, a waking experience was at the root of a complete emotional transformation for Cindy Walters. At the time of her experience she was nineteen years old, the youngest of seven children and had a father and a stepmother who loved her. By all accounts Cindy had a good life and much to be thankful for. She was away at college for the summer when she experienced a personal encounter with the Divine, but the roots of her experience had begun years earlier.

Her mother had died due to the complications of Cindy's birth. It was a subject that no one in her family ever wanted to discuss. As a result, for as long as she could remember, she felt that something was missing from her life. As a child she had often shared her feelings with her siblings about how much she missed their mother, but their response had always been, "You didn't even know her. How could you miss her?" Even though she truly loved her brothers and sisters, that statement always made her extremely angry: How could they even know what it was like? Her father had remarried and had a wonderful wife—a friend of Cindy's mother—but still Cindy couldn't help how she felt. There was an emptiness in her life that would not go away. She wanted a ring, a picture, or something that belonged to her mother, but she had nothing.

One night while Cindy was sitting outside at school looking at the beauty of her surroundings, her thoughts turned once again to the mother she had never known. The longer she sat there, the sadder she became. Eventually, all of her pent-up anger and loneliness seemed to flow:

Why did her mother have to die? Why couldn't the family talk about it . . . Why couldn't I have anything of hers? Something that was special and meaningful to her—something that she cherished? I MISS HER TOO! My brothers and sister missed what they had. At least they had it! Does anyone know how painful this is?

Clouds had covered the moon, and Cindy found herself sitting alone in darkness, sobbing. She shed tears of sadness and of anger. She felt much pain while her tears continued to fall. All of a sudden, without explanation or reason, she felt a peace descend upon her. She felt a Divine presence, and her tears of anger became "tears of cleansing." Cindy is convinced that she heard God speak to her that night:

"Sweet child, you do have what was most precious to her. You have what she looked at and touched daily. You have what she loved the most . . . Your brothers and sisters were the things that were most precious to her."

Slowly the moon began to peek out from behind the clouds, and her surroundings were filled with a heavenly light as He continued:

"Your mother loved them and cherished them far more than any ring. They're better than a picture. To look at them is to look at and be with her. You've always had what you've wanted most . . . You have her in them. You have her in her good friend, your stepmother; you have her in your father. Pain can block love; try to let it go. Embrace the love."

Through her tears, Cindy became aware of the fact that she felt cleansed and full of love. When her tears ended, the moon was full, and she felt uplifted by what had happened.

That one encounter became a transformational experience that truly changed her perception. Even now, twenty years later, Cindy looks back on that evening and states positively, "I have been different ever since—more grateful for *all of life*, for the love, for the trials, for the joys and for the pain." Although she has not experienced the voice again, ever since that time she is convinced that she is not alone when her life seems troubled by personal challenges. Even in the face of them she strives to be gentle, kind and loving: "I have come to know that people and relationships are what matter most, not things. Relationships are to be honored and cherished, because they can be fragile."

Each of these contemporary encounters with the Divine happened to ordinary people in the course of their regular lives. All of these experiences had an impact on the individual that lasted even decades after the experience was over. Each of these individuals became convinced that somehow the Divine had intervened or at least made Itself known in their lives. In spite of even the most remarkable of claims, these accounts are not isolated instances. They are simply a few of the innumerable ways in which God has reportedly become involved in people's lives through health, through dreams, through life's challenges, through nature, through death and through innumerable other instances. Together they may make the surprising assertion that perhaps we are never truly alone.

2

Healing Experiences

Know ye not that there are more nations than one? Know ye not that I, the Lord your God, have created all men, and that I remember those who are upon the isles of the sea; and that I rule in the heavens above and in the earth beneath; and I bring forth my word unto the children of men, yea, even upon all the nations of the earth?

The Book of Mormon
2 Nephi 29:7

Francesco Forgione was born in obscurity to simple farming parents in a little village in southern Italy on May 25, 1887. One of eight children—five of whom would survive infancy—Francesco was a sickly, quiet and devout youth. In spite of the poverty and simplicity into which he was born, his life would leave a lasting impression on his village and on Catholicism. He was said to be a man in constant communication with the Divine—one whose faith was unswerving. Although he never traveled far from his birthplace, in time his fame would spread worldwide. Literally dozens of books have been written about his life. When he died in September 1968, his funeral attracted approximately 100,000 mourners. The Catholic Church began the process for sainthood less than five years after his death, for this child of simple farmers had gained recognition far beyond his humble beginnings. At the age of twenty-two Francesco had become a priest and had taken the name Padre Pio—a man who would become associated with hundreds of healing miracles.

Even at the age of five, Francesco's parents had noticed the boy's piety and devotion. At the age of ten, Francesco announced that he wanted to be a friar. When he was fifteen, he applied for entrance into the Capuchin order of friars and took the name *Pio* in honor of Saint Pius V, the patron saint of the city of his birth. In spite of feeble health as a youth, he took his final vows as a friar in 1907 and was ordained a priest three years later.

Within a month of his ordination, Padre Pio was praying in a chapel when reportedly both Jesus and Mary appeared to him. During the vision he received the stigmata—open wounds in the palms of his hands, his feet and his side, all resembling the crucifixion marks of Jesus. Doctors could find no cause for the wounds, and Padre Pio sought to conceal them from others by wearing gloves or woolen mittens. Soon thereafter the wounds disappeared. However, within a year he became very ill and was thought to be on the verge of death. His condition was eventually diagnosed as tuberculosis. For that reason he was sent home, where he remained for five years. In spite of his ongoing illness, when Pio was well enough, he said Mass and taught school.

In 1918 the stigmata wounds returned and would remain for the next fifty years. With the reappearance of the stigmata, Padre Pio was again examined by doctors who found no explanation for the wounds, nor could they find any trace of the tuberculosis. The disappearance of the tuberculosis seemed miraculous, enabling Pio to return to his duties as a priest. However, the appearance of the stigmata and the notoriety that eventually resulted caused the Catholic Church a great deal of concern. For more than ten years he would come under the close scrutiny of the Church and his superiors. The wounds did not heal; they never stopped bleeding; they did not become worse, nor did they ever become infected. At night his hands bled constantly, causing him to wear fingerless mittens most of the time. The daily loss of blood equaled approximately a small teacup. At times the pain in his hands was so severe that he could hardly turn the pages of a book while saying Mass. Because of the wounds in his feet, he also had difficulty walking. However, in spite of his constant pain, he was never heard to complain, nor did his devotion and faithfulness ever waver. Throughout his life he would be known as a deeply religious man of God—one that could intercede with the Divine for countless individuals through the power of prayer.

Another unexplainable phenomenon associated with Padre Pio was that the blood from his wounds often emanated the scent of perfume. The perfume was likened unto the smell of violets, roses, incense, lilies, carnations, or—on occasion—fresh tobacco. The scent of the perfume was pronounced, and Padre Pio did not even need to be in the same room with an individual for her or him to notice it. In time, its scent would become associated with his presence, his prayers and his comfort, or the fact that some miracle of healing was about to be bestowed through his intercession. Doctor Romanelli of Barletta, one of the first doctors to examine Padre Pio's stigmata, eventually reported:

> In June 1919, on my first visit to Padre Pio, I noticed a peculiar scent, so much so that I said to Father Valenzano who was with me at the time that I thought it very unsuitable for a friar to use perfume . . . it is impossible for blood to give out a sweet odor, but the blood that drips from the stigmata of Padre Pio has a characteristic one, which even those who have no sense of smell can detect. Besides which, when the blood is coagulated, or dried on some garment that he has worn, it still retains its perfume.
>
> Carty, 35–36

In addition to his visionary encounters and his stigmata, Padre Pio claimed that he could also speak with angels. In 1919, in order to test the validity of Padre Pio's claims, one of his superiors wrote a letter to him in Greek—a language totally unknown to the young priest. When Pio was able to understand what had been written, however, his superior asked how that was possible, and the younger priest stated, "My guardian angel explained it all to me." (Parente, 32) Later in life Pio would have similar experiences, appearing to understand spoken or written languages of which he had no conscious knowledge.

In order to maintain his connection with the Divine, Padre Pio was known to pray for extended periods of time. For his own attunement each day before saying Mass, Pio spent several hours in prayer and meditation. Afterwards, he was known to hear confessions for as long as eighteen hours a day. By all accounts, his spiritual devotion enabled him to perfectly console and guide those who came to him, bringing them peace and tranquility in the process.

Because of the ever-present stigmata and the rumors of his ability to heal, Padre Pio's fame began to spread, causing no small disruption in the simple monastic life at San Giovanni Rotondo where he worked. In order to put an end to the ever-increasing crowds who sought his presence, between 1931 and 1933 his superiors withheld him from public audiences, not allowing him to hear confessions or say Mass in public. In spite of Pio's virtual imprisonment, however, numerous individuals including priests allegedly witnessed Padre Pio's miraculous ability to appear and disappear from any location at will. As a result, the priest's seclusion was eventually suspended.

One story associated with his ability to transport himself occurred during World War II, when Padre Pio assured the people of San Giovanni Rotondo that their town would not be bombed. At the time, the Americans had an airbase about seventy-five miles away from the city. Rumors persisted that the Germans had established a munitions dump in or near San Giovanni Rotondo. For that reason, the American forces had planned an air raid on the town. According to the story, when the planes neared the area, the officer in charge of the raid suddenly saw a monk floating in the air in front of his plane with arms outstretched—apparently blocking the plane's path to the city. Surprised, shocked and convinced that he was either losing his mind or suffering from mental fatigue, the officer called off the mission and ordered the bombs dropped in an open field. When the officer returned to the base and described what he had seen, an Italian officer told him there was a monk in the town that the locals considered a saint—reportedly the monk could work miracles. Determined to prove whether or not his eyes had been playing tricks on him, the American officer went to the town to see the monk in question. When he saw Padre Pio, he immediately recognized the monk as the individual he had seen in the sky. (Carty, 24)

This phenomenon of observing Padre Pio's body in a place that he could not possibly be was not an isolated incidence. Repeatedly, individuals described Pio's ability to bilocate—possessing the power to be in two places at once. One of dozens of examples occurred in the case of a Mrs. Devota of Genoa, who was seriously ill and was scheduled to have one of her legs amputated.

Mrs. Devota's daughter knew of Padre Pio and decided to pray to him since San Giovanni Rotondo was hundreds of miles away and it would not be possible for the priest to come in person. Fearful of her mother's pending operation, the daughter prayed in the hospital room that the operation would not have to happen and that Padre Pio could somehow intercede on their behalf. For some time the woman prayed. Suddenly, she felt the presence of someone in the room. When she looked up and opened her eyes, she was amazed to see Padre Pio standing in the doorway. She begged him, "Oh, Father, save my dear mother." The priest replied, "Wait for nine days." When the woman looked back in the direction of the doorway, the priest was gone.

The next day the woman informed the doctors that her mother's operation had to be postponed for nine days. The doctors protested, saying that the operation had to be performed as soon as possible. Nonetheless, she insisted and the operation was postponed. On the tenth day when the doctors came to visit the elderly woman's room, they found that her leg was completely healed and that the operation was no longer necessary. (Carty, 63–64) It would become one of literally hundreds of healing miracles eventually associated with the priest.

Padre Pio became known for his loving kindness and his ability to bring comfort to thousands. During his lifetime, individuals who were sincere in asking for his help or guidance became his "spiritual children." Pio often encouraged these individuals to simply "Send Me Your Guardian Angel" whenever they were in need of his help or spiritual assistance. One of these spiritual children was English gentleman, speaker and author Cecil Humphrey-Smith, who often had the opportunity to visit Padre Pio at San Giovanni Rotondo.

According to reports, one day Humphrey-Smith was seriously injured in a car accident far away from San Giovanni Rotondo and his friend the priest. Concerned about the injuries, another friend of Smith's went to the post office to send a telegram to Padre Pio asking for prayers. To the friend's surprise when he reached the post office, there was a telegram from Padre Pio to Cecil Humphrey-Smith assuring him that he would be prayed for. Months later, when Cecil Humphrey-Smith had recovered and found occasion to visit Padre Pio in person, he asked how the priest had known about the accident, to which Padre Pio replied: "Do you think the angels go as slowly as the planes?" (Parente, 81)

On another occasion, a woman had given birth to a healthy baby girl. However, at five weeks the child developed a cold, which became pneumonia. The child was medicated and hospitalized and her condition continued to worsen. The baby started to lose body fluid and was not responding to treatment. As the situation deteriorated, the child was placed in an incubator, and the parents were told that there was no longer any hope—they needed to prepare for the inevitable death of their infant child.

In desperation, the mother placed her arms around the incubator and cried out to her guardian angel to take a message to Padre Pio, "to make my baby live." The mother thought she saw the child shiver slightly at her words, but the next morning there was no change in the baby's condition. The mother repeated her words from the night before. Miraculously, by six o'clock in the evening the doctors themselves had noticed a slight improvement in the child. Four weeks later the baby had fully recovered and was sent home. (Parente, 141–142)

In 1950 one of Pio's healing miracles would receive widespread attention in several Italian newspapers, only adding to the priest's fame. The case was that of a ten-year-old boy who was diagnosed with heart disease and was not expected to live. The disease had caused extensive swelling throughout the child's body. Several doctors had given the same prognosis: the child would die. According to the reports, one evening the child pleaded in a very weak voice for his father to seek out the help of Padre Pio and ask for a cure. The father replied that he would go the next day to San Giovanni Rotondo. The child begged his father to leave that very night, for apparently there was no time to waste. The father followed his son's request and arrived at San Giovanni Rotondo monastery late that evening and received an audience with the priest.

Before the father could even explain why he had come, Padre Pio assured him that his son would be cured. As they discussed the situation, three times the priest assured the boy's father that everything would be okay, the third time adding that in about two months time the child would be completely recovered.

When the father returned to the hospital, he learned from his son that during the evening the boy had had a dream. While the boy slept, Padre Pio had apparently appeared to the child as a reassuring presence. The boy told his father that he could see the priest's hands bleeding from the stigmata. Immediately thereafter, the swelling in the child's body, as well as his heart condition, inexplicably began to improve. Two months later, the doctors' prognosis had completely changed: the boy was expected to make a full recovery.

On another occasion, a woman's three-year-old granddaughter was diagnosed with infantile paralysis. In spite of three months of treatment and the concerted efforts of doctors, medical professors and specialists, the condition of the child showed no improvement. After various treatments, medicines, x-rays and electrical stimulation, the child retained only some movement in her neck. Understandably, the parents were heartbroken and began to wonder whether or not it might be better for their daughter to die rather than to spend the rest of her life in bed, completely paralyzed.

Without telling the family, the grandmother made a trip to the monastery at San Giovanni Rotondo. Not knowing whether or not she would have the opportunity to meet Padre Pio, after her arrival she found that the priest was hearing confessions, and she waited her turn. As soon as she entered the confessional and before she could even speak, Padre Pio reportedly asked her, "You have come for the baby?" The grandmother began to sob, and before she could say a word, the priest assured her, "Go home, go home, you will find your baby better. Take courage, pray to our Lord for the cure."

When she returned home several days later, she was greeted with the news that while she had been away, the child had miraculously sat up in her bed—the miracle had occurred at the same moment she had been in the confessional with Padre Pio. From that day forward, the child improved until she was completely normal. When the child was five and a half years old, the grandmother reported, "She is robust, healthy, very bright and very pious, [and] she never forgets Padre Pio . . . " (Carty, 221–223)

One of the most amazing cures on record occurred to a young laborer named Giovanni Savino, who had been dynamiting rocks in the monastery gardens at San Giovanni Rotondo. One day, a small charge exploded in Savino's face. He was taken to the hospital, where doctors discovered that his right eye had been blown out of its socket and his left eye was so badly damaged with rock fragments that no one expected Savino to be able to see again.

According to Savino, one night while he was in the hospital, Padre Pio came to him and slapped him slightly on the right side of the head. Miraculously, a few days later Savino could see out of his right eye—an eye that the doctors said no longer existed. When Savino went to the monastery to thank Padre Pio for the healing slap, the priest smiled and said, "Here is another one" and slapped him gently on the left side of his face. Afterwards, Savino could see out of both eyes and did not even require the use of glasses. (Carty, 232-233)

Because of his notoriety, Padre Pio was able to begin a building fund to construct a modern-day hospital for healing. By 1956 Padre had managed to chair the collection of more than $6 million dollars, and the hospital was built. Called the *House for the Relief of Suffering*, locals referred to it simply as "Padre Pio's hospital."

During the 1960s, Pio received between 600 and 800 letters a day and an additional 50 to 80 telegrams. Letters would come to him in Italian, English, French, German, Hungarian, Latin, Spanish and Portuguese. Although unable to answer any of these letters himself, Padre Pio would pray for the writers, and a staff of secretaries fluent in the respective language would acknowledge their petitions and assure them of his prayers.

Throughout his life, Pio was revered for his piety and devotion. While saying Mass, he often seemed to be in a state of spiritual ecstasy—appearing as one transfigured. He was known for his ability to speak with angels and to send the healing power of the Divine to individuals around the globe. Padre Pio's faith and devotion seemed to act as some sort of transmitter, bringing spiritual energy into the material world. Hundreds of healing miracles are associated with him and include cures for diphtheria, hernias, heart disease, bone fractures, the inability to conceive, arthritis, cancer, pneumonia, stomach ulcers, diabetes, tuberculosis, infantile paralysis and even blindness.

Padre Pio carried the stigmata until his death in 1968. After his passing, the wounds miraculously healed. The process for sainthood was begun by the Church five years later, and on May 2, 1999, Pope John Paul II beatified Padre Pio, recognizing him as "Blessed Pio of Pietrelcina." It was once said of Padre Pio's life, "To those who believe, it will increase their faith; to those who do not believe, they will at least begin to wonder." (Parente, 4)

■

In another contemporary example of the healing power of prayer, Horst and Helene Gudren are convinced that prayer and Divine intervention averted what might have become a parent's worst nightmare. In their thirties, the couple was living in Indiana about one-half mile from the highway connecting Indianapolis with Louisville. Parents with a two-year-old son and a three-year-old daughter, they had a relative visiting that summer with another three-year-old child.

As Horst remembers the story, the afternoon was like any other. Helene busied herself in the kitchen and watched the children playing out back in their sandbox while Horst was working at the nearby auto dealership. Suddenly, one of the salesmen ran into the auto showroom and screamed that there had just been a hit and run accident out by the highway. Apparently, a little boy wearing bright red sneakers had been run over by a car and had been found by an off-duty deputy sheriff who had just called an ambulance to rush the child to the hospital.

All at once Horst was terrified because the day before, he and Helene had bought their two-year-old son, Matthew, a new pair of red sneakers. He picked up the phone and called Helene, who was panicked to find that the children were missing. He hurried home immediately and arrived just as a Good Samaritan was dropping two three-year-olds off at the house. Horst's little boy was missing—the red-sneakered child had been his son. Horst soon discovered that Helene had rushed to the site of the accident and was taken with Matthew in the ambulance to the nearby hospital.

When Horst got inside the house, the phone was ringing. Helene was calling from the hospital and said that Matthew's head injuries were so severe that they required transfer to Indianapolis Methodist Hospital. She would go with their son, and Horst needed to find someone to watch the kids and come in the car as soon as possible.

Neighbors were quickly called to come over and watch the children. As soon as they arrived, Horst left the house and drove as fast as he could in what he describes as "my worst drive ever . . . praying all the way for our two-year-old whose life had barely begun." Unbeknownst to Horst or Helene, while Horst was on his way, the neighbors he had left the children with had called other friends and neighbors, and a large prayer circle was forming in their home. The group brought together food and drink and planned to pray for Matthew late into the evening.

When Horst got to the hospital, he heard the horrifying diagnosis: a compound depressed skull fracture calling for surgery and the relocation of damaged parts of the skull to relieve pressure on the brain and avoid brain damage. The injuries were very serious, and Matthew was in surgery for five hours. Horst and Helene waited in the hospital room, worried, hoped and prayed.

To their surprise, the next morning Matthew was brought back to the room, "not in a bed or a stretcher but on the arm of a nurse, wide awake and alert, and hollering for water." The couple fell into each other's arms, crying tears of joy and thanking God for the outcome. Their son appeared completely normal with no adverse signs from the accident. To everyone's joy and surprise, Matthew was discharged several days later.

The couple is convinced that their prayers, the prayers of their friends and neighbors, and the quick work of the deputy sheriff who arrived at the scene right after Matthew had been hit were all responsible for their child's survival. Their little boy grew up like any other child except for a scar on the right side of his head—an imprint from the right front bumper of the car that had hit him. The driver of the hit and run was never located, but Horst and Helene are grateful that somehow they became privy to a miracle.

■

Another case of prayer resulting in instantaneous healing is the story of Anne Ellis, who has worked with meditation and the power of healing prayer for years. While getting ready for a dinner party, Anne was preparing taco shells in hot peanut oil—frying them in 375-degree oil.

When she had completed frying all of the shells, she unplugged the deep fryer and carried it from the stove to the sink. Before she reached the sink, however, one of the handles on the fryer broke off, causing all of the hot oil to fall onto her legs and knees. Anne screamed out as her legs buckled and she fell to the floor, causing further burns as her hands fell into the oil.

Anne's husband and a friend ran into the kitchen just as she was pulling herself up. Her legs were scalded red and throbbing with pain—blisters had already started to form. Her husband wanted to take her to the hospital but she insisted that there were too many people coming to the party. She told him, "You clean up the mess; I will go and pray." Anne described what happened next:

I kept thinking, "I don't want to go to the hospital. I don't have time to go to the hospital." I went into my bedroom and set down in my meditation chair. I started praying immediately, asking for a healing, while doing the laying-on-of-hands on myself. My legs were beet red, and so were the palms of my hands and knees. My legs were so tender and throbbing that I couldn't even touch them. I simply held my hands above my legs and prayed fervently, knowing that I could be healed.

As I prayed, I told my body that it could eliminate the injured tissue. I knew that prayer would make it possible for the blood stream to remove any damaged tissues and that the cells could regenerate themselves. I repeatedly moved my hands above the red areas of my legs and prayed.

Within minutes the pain began to subside. I gave thanks for the Divine healing that was taking place. As the pain began to diminish, I imagined that the redness and the blisters were beginning to disappear. After my legs and knees had responded to the prayers, I held my palms about a quarter-inch apart from one another and prayed that they might be healed, as well.

When Anne's husband came to check on her, he was amazed to find that her knees, hands and legs appeared completely normal: no burns, no redness, no blisters. According to Anne, "I got up, wiped off my hands and legs and finished getting things ready for dinner." No one at the party knew what had happened except for her husband and the friend who had seen the burns. She has no doubt that prayer brought about a miraculous healing.

■

Another healing miracle occurred in the life of Jennifer Barnes in 1954 at the age of fifteen. Just before the Salk vaccine became available, Jennifer contracted polio. In those days it was difficult to diagnose polio from spinal meningitis, so she was kept at home for observation. However, within three weeks her condition had worsened so much that it became clear she had polio and required hospitalization.

Jennifer's parents were disheartened and depressed by the tragic news that their daughter was paralyzed from the waist down. Doctors had performed a lumbar puncture and diagnosed the presence of bulbar polio—the most serious kind. Her parents prayed for her recovery, but still Jennifer's condition deteriorated. A few weeks later, the girl had become so ill that doctors decided the time had come to put her in an iron lung. Desperate and not knowing what else to do, her parents phoned an Episcopal priest who reportedly had the gift of healing. He was forty miles away but promised to do an absentee healing by praying through the night. He advised Jennifer's parents to spend that time affirming their love and faith in God.

To everyone's surprise, the next morning Jennifer opened her eyes and sat up in bed. She insisted on trying to walk and with help was able to get up out of bed and walk a distance of about three feet. The medical staff declared that the diagnosis had been inaccurate because a recovery of such magnitude "was not possible." A second lumbar puncture, however, confirmed the presence of the polio virus. Doctors had to concede that somehow Jennifer had recovered from the disease, and her medical file was eventually placed in the "unexplained" annals of the hospital records.

Amazingly, Jennifer experienced a complete recovery. Her experience was eventually detailed in *Guidepost* magazine. It also inspired her and her parents to begin a spiritual journey that went beyond their traditional religious backgrounds. She became a member of Unity Church and worked with healing others through a career in nursing.

Now retired with two grown children and two grandchildren, Jennifer believes her healing experience helped to contribute to an understanding of her place in the universe and her true connection to the Divine. Today, Jennifer describes her spiritual beliefs, as follows:

> There is no place in my life for prejudice or conditional love. Every thought, word and deed creates an indelible effect on the Universe. My God is pure love in the form of Divine energy that permeates all animate and inanimate life and objects. I feel a strong and constant connection to the Divine Presence within me, and a love for all creation.

■

Suzanne Hansen is another individual who has experienced a miracle of healing in her life. Although she still considers herself too critical and prone to have a temper and a quick tongue, Suzanne is convinced that in spite of her imperfections a Divine encounter saved her from a life of partial paralysis. Setting the stage for her "miracle," Suzanne describes herself as a wife and mother of one young daughter. Her second pregnancy went well enough up until the time of the delivery. While she was in the delivery room, the doctor gave her an epidural to block the pain. Unfortunately during the procedure, part of the needle broke off in her spine. After giving birth to a second daughter, Suzanne found out that she had partial paralysis in her legs and a constant pain in her spine. It was a condition she would have to endure for several years.

In order to help alleviate the condition, another physician had given Suzanne some painful physiotherapy exercises that she performed dutifully for years. The exercises helped her recovery somewhat; however, the pain persisted, and Suzanne was subjected to frequent falls because of the paralysis in her legs.

Throughout her suffering, Suzanne worried most about her youngest daughter. The girl seemed to fear for her mother's condition and was anxious every time Suzanne fell or seemed to be in pain. The whole experience proved frightening to the young child. One day in the midst of Suzanne's physiotherapy exercises, she "talked to God about having more faith than a grain of mustard seed." She believed that she had enough faith to help heal her condition. After her conversation with

God, she became witness to a vision:

Jesus came. At first I saw his face off in the distance. His face came closer and closer until I got lost in His eyes. All at once I forgot my surroundings, and I saw beautiful rivers and valleys, trees and streams. I was overwhelmed by his presence and my surroundings until I remembered that I was actually in the living room doing my exercises. All at once, I found myself back in the living room, and He was gone.

To her amazement, after the encounter Suzanne found that her pain and her paralysis were both completely gone. The healing was not temporary but persisted. Even now, years later, she has not experienced the pain or the paralysis again. In reflecting back on her life, Suzanne states simply, "I wish I were better for all I have been given . . . I have been so blessed."

■

In another example, Evelyn Carter understands that her story might sound unusual to some because her experience with the Divine enabled her to heal herself emotionally—even in the face of her husband's untimely and tragic death:

I was in my late twenties. At the time, my husband had been diagnosed with terminal cancer. Although we had faced and struggled with this illness for years, we had just learned it had entered a terminal state. I was very depressed and was not sure I could go on to see this situation through. I just wanted to give up.

Evelyn was under a great deal of stress and unhappiness. She felt that her own sense of selfhood was eighty percent identified with her husband and that if he died "I had little reason to continue." One reason that she had to keep some semblance of normalcy going was the fact that the couple had a five-year-old daughter. However, her determination was tested repeatedly because her husband had to undergo one surgery after another to remove cancerous tissue. Her husband's slow demise at the age of thirty proved to be a very difficult process—painful for him, horrible to watch, difficult to bear. To her surprise, one night while she was lying in bed, she became aware of several "spirit voices" or angels speaking about her wellbeing:

> They were discussing the state of my emotional and mental consciousness and whether I had the ability or strength to continue. It sounded like some of the beings were not sure I had it in me to continue while others had no doubt I could make it. About that time, I became aware of a light in the distance. I felt only love and support coming from this bright light . . . the voices kept encouraging me, saying, "You can do this Evelyn. Keep trying. You have the strength."

Her husband's struggle continued for several months, and still Evelyn forced herself to deal with life, her job, a dying husband confined to bed, a five-year-old daughter and her own despondency. It was not easy, but Evelyn somehow managed to deal with the trauma and stress of the experience. A few months later, a second encounter provided her with additional encouragement:

> I was asleep and awoke to find a very bright light at the foot of my bed. I closed my eyes and opened them a few times. I even switched my position in bed to see if the light or its intensity diminished. Neither changed. As I stared at the light, I received a wonderful feeling of comfort, love and encouragement. I stayed in the state of suspended animation meditation with the light for about five minutes.

The light provided Evelyn with the support she needed when her husband finally succumbed to death. The final stages of his illness forced her to depend upon her spiritual life and to form a new identity for herself. Evelyn says that the entire experience "marked a turning point in my life." She is convinced that the person she is today would have been inconceivable to her at the time of her Divine encounters and her husband's passing. After his death, she went back to school and earned a master's degree in health administration. She was able to go to school while raising her daughter as a single parent. Today, she is an executive vice president and administrator for a large hospital system. As difficult as the experience proved to be, Evelyn understands how it helped her to grow as a person, to overcome her sense of dependency and to realize that she was much more than simply a wife and a mother.

■

A more successful outcome with cancer occurred in the story of Candace Roberts and her boyfriend Mike. An engineer by profession, Mike was both funny and clever, but he was also subject to fits of depression—a condition that tended to make their relationship rocky. Although Candace had been raised with a Presbyterian background, Mike did not have any belief in God. When he was diagnosed with a rare form of cancer, it was Candace who felt that she was in spiritual distress.

According to the doctors, Mike's only hope of survival was surgery. The prognosis caused Mike's depression to worsen. He became convinced that even if he survived the operation, the cancer would kill him eventually. According to Candace, during the illness she became his caretaker, his support and his primary cheerleader:

> Although I was never a maternal person and had no experience nursing anyone, I took care of him for the duration of his illness. I stuffed him full of organic produce and supplements so he would be strong for the surgery. I listened to his fears and concerns and gave wise counsel. Something bigger than I was meeting this enormous challenge, and I knew it and was awed. Somehow I knew the right things to say and do, just like my mother always did in a crisis. For the first time, I was loving someone unconditionally and experiencing a joy in service that I'd never known.
>
> Oh, how I prayed for Mike's recovery and for my own strength! And how I thanked God for the strength He had given me to help.

In spite of the fact that Mike's surgery went well and doctors felt optimistic about a recovery, Mike remained convinced that he was going to die. His depression worsened. He often stated that the cancer was going to come back and kill him. There was no convincing him otherwise; Mike was certain his life was coming to an end.

After weeks of Mike's depression and his repeated statements that he was dying, Candace began to wonder if Mike was correct after all. She could no longer maintain her sense of optimism. Perhaps Mike was intuiting the real outcome and her own sense of hope was blinding her to the truth. She started to feel depressed and wondered whether she was doing her boyfriend a disservice by repeatedly insisting that everything was going to be okay. One day she was in Mike's room praying hard for him and praying for her own strength to continue: "Poor Mike. He was so convinced that he was going to die that I was starting to believe him." All at once, Candace heard a voice:

> Having heard about the biblical "still, small voice," I have to say there was nothing small about this voice. It was a huge thought that bloomed full-grown in my head and filled my entire being. It rang with authority but also with love. It opened me up even more to knowing the Creator as a loving force . . . The voice filled my whole self: "HE WILL BE ALL RIGHT! DO NOT FEAR! EVERYTHING IS GOING TO BE ALL RIGHT!

There was no mistaking the authority in those words, or the boundless love and compassion that flowed through them.

The voice proved correct. Mike survived, and ten years later there is no sign of the cancer. Eventually, however, the couple broke up and went on with their respective lives. Candace states that Mike never did have a spiritual transformation because of his experience; however, she did: "What I didn't expect was the conversion that took place within me. My life, by being of service in genuine love, was changed forever. I had found joy in service that I never wanted to have end." Even now, Candace looks for ways in which she can reach out and be of service to others.

■

Describing herself as a "free thinker and a free spirit" in terms of her spiritual beliefs, Terry Marks tells of a healing experience that occurred for her husband after a near-fatal car accident. At the time of the accident, she and her husband were having difficulties, in part because he had gone into business against her wishes with a partner she didn't trust. The couple was also having financial problems. Terry labels that stage of their marriage as simply "very difficult times."

The accident was so severe that it was feared her husband would not survive. In fact, Terry later discovered that her husband had experienced a Near Death Experience while in surgery. The surgery lasted eight hours, and afterwards her husband was admitted to the ICU. When he had stabilized, Terry took a short break from the hospital. On her way back, she found herself praying in the car:

I prayed and asked if he was going to recover somehow, in spite of the seriousness of the accident. I kept praying, wondering what was going to happen to us. My answer came just as I exited the interstate and headed toward the hospital:

All at once, a shaft of light in rainbow colors appeared in front of me. As soon as I saw the rainbow, I felt comforted. A feeling of peace replaced my worries and concerns. I somehow knew beyond any doubt that he was going to recover. I knew that we were going to be given a second chance.

True to her feelings, Terry's husband did make a full recovery. Afterwards, the couple made some positive changes in their lives. They worked through their problems. Terry worked at not being so judgmental of others—including her husband's partner. Her husband worked at seeing their marriage as his first priority and most important partnership. They worked at forgiving one another for those things that were not of greatest significance after all. As a result, their marriage has become even better than before the accident. Terry affirms: "The accident made both of us not ever take one another for granted because we realized that in an instant or a twinkling of an eye our whole relationship could be lost. It made us realize what was really important."

■

For Rachel Adams a persistent problem with an ovarian cyst finally led to the conclusion that surgery was inevitable. Always open to new ideas, Rachel's religious background included growing up Catholic, spending time with both the Baptist and the Mormon faiths and studying the Far East teachings of the Ascended Masters. That openness also caused her to pursue a variety of non-traditional treatments for her cyst without success.

At the time, Rachel's husband was working overseas, and she was living in the Texas countryside with two teenage children and working in various parts of the state. Because of her job and her children, any stay in the hospital was out of the question. However, when the pain from her cyst became unbearable and she felt she had exhausted all other options, Rachel found a doctor in Austin—ninety minutes away—who would perform the surgery and then release her.

Plans did not go as well as she had expected. On the way to Austin, her car broke down, plus when she arrived at the hospital, the admissions desk insisted on a $1,000 deposit—money she did not have. Still in pain, Rachel argued with admissions, persisting until the hospital finally agreed to admit her.

When she headed for surgery, the doctor was surprised that Rachel refused anything but a local for the pain. Her rationale was that her hectic schedule did not allow for unnecessary recovery time: "I knew that I couldn't take anything and still be able to drive myself home that night. I also knew that I had a three-and-a-half-hour drive the next morning to go to work in Houston."

After the surgery, Rachel managed to drive home. She was tired, still in pain and emotionally exhausted. When she finally got into her own bed, she cried and pleaded for help: "Dear God! Please God! May I be healed once and for all of this. I beg you!" Afterwards, she was completely worn out and fell fast asleep.

Rachel was startled awake at 4:30 a.m. when she felt something brush up against her knee. At the same time she heard "an incredible swishing sound." She immediately opened her eyes and saw two huge pairs of angelic wings disappearing into the ceiling above her. She clearly saw two Divine messengers leaving her bedroom. Although amazed, Rachel had no doubt she had been visited by two angels and that her prayers had been answered. She also realized that in spite of the surgery, she had awakened without any pain. Even later, pain was absent, and she never again had any problems.

In retrospect, Rachel says that she is glad that she didn't take a sedative for her pain or stay overnight in the hospital. In addition to having no one who could have stayed out in the country with her children and having no easy way to cancel her commitment in Houston, had she done what the doctor wanted, she would have missed a most amazing encounter with the Divine:

"Had I taken the pain medication, I feel it would have been unlikely that I would have even seen the angels"—angels that came in answer to a prayer.

3

Divine Encounters in Dreams

For this commandment which I command thee this day, it is not hidden from thee, neither is it far off. It is not in heaven, that thou shouldest say, Who shall go up for us to heaven, and bring it unto us, that we may hear it, and do it? Neither is it beyond the sea, that thou shouldest say, who shall go over the sea for us, and bring it unto us, that we may hear it, and do it? But the word is very nigh unto thee, in thy mouth, and in thy heart, that thou mayest do it.

The Holy Bible
Deuteronomy 30:11–14

For thousands of years cultural and religious traditions held to the belief that the Divine could communicate to individuals through the dream state. This belief has had a profound influence on many diverse traditions throughout the world. In the Old Testament, Hebrew prophets such as Jacob, Joseph and Daniel rose to prominence because of their ability to interpret dreams and thereby understand and relate the Will of God.

It was through a dream that Jacob received a message from the Divine that his descendents would become as plentiful "as the dust of the earth." (Genesis 28:14) Later, God would change his name to *Israel*, establishing Jacob as the patriarch of the Twelve Tribes of the Hebrew nation. Jacob's favorite son, Joseph, would also rise to prominence in the kingdom of Egypt because of his ability to interpret dreams.

According to Genesis 41, the Egyptian Pharaoh was troubled by a dream of seven fat cows coming up out of the Nile followed by seven thin cows that ate the fat cows. The dream apparently came as a nightmare, causing the Pharaoh to awaken. Later that same night, the Pharaoh had a second troubling dream in which seven fat ears of corn grew only to be devoured by seven thin ears. The second dream caused the ruler to awaken in fright, as well.

Deeply distressed by these dreams, the Pharaoh summoned all of the wise men and magicians of Egypt to assist him in understanding them. Unfortunately, no one could interpret the dreams to Pharaoh's satisfaction. It was then that Joseph—a man with a knack for dream interpretation who had been wrongfully imprisoned for something he had not done—was brought to the ruler's attention. Joseph comforted the Pharaoh by explaining that the dreams were a message from God and provided the ruler with information to help govern the land: Egypt would experience seven years of plenty, followed by seven years of famine. Because of Joseph's ability to understand the Divine Will, the Pharaoh released him from prison and placed him second in command of the Egyptian nation as a means of preparing for what was to come.

Later, another powerful ruler, Nebuchadnezzar, the king of Babylon who had destroyed Jerusalem and held captive many of the Jews, was troubled by his own dreams. As in the case of the Pharaoh, Nebuchadnezzar called together all of the wise men, sorcerers and astrologers of his kingdom. However, the nightmares that bothered the king's sleep were so troubling that he could not even remember their content upon awakening. As a means of deducing his wise men's interpretative abilities, Nebuchadnezzar wanted them not only to interpret the dreams but to describe what the forgotten dreams had been about in the first place. In spite of the threat of death, the wise men refused, stating that "there is not a man upon the earth" that possessed such abilities. (Daniel 2:10) Only Daniel proved up to the task. After praying to God for assistance, the secret and meaning of Nebuchadnezzar's dreams were revealed to Daniel in "a night vision" of his own. As a result, Nebuchadnezzar accepted Daniel's god as a "God of gods" and appointed Daniel the ruler of Babylon and chief of the kingdom's wise men. (Daniel 2:47–48)

In the ancient Egypt and Mesopotamian cultures, dreams were often considered to be messages from the gods. The Sumerian king Gudea (ca.

2200 B.C.), who has been called "the first known historical figure associated with a dream," wished to build a temple to his god, Nin-Girsu. Through a series of dreams that provided encouragement, chastisement and even interpretation of previous dreams, Gudea received guidance for his proposed temple to the god. (Van de Castle, 49) Another example of a Divine dream dating to the time of the Egyptian King Thutmoses IV (1401–1391 B.C.), exists in the form of a stone tablet between the paws of the Great Sphinx that tells how a dream was responsible for Thutmoses' rise to power:

> When Thutmoses was a youth, the Sphinx had been neglected and was covered with sand to its neck. One day the prince slept in the shadow of its head and had a dream. In the dream, the Sphinx told him, "Son, gaze your eyes upon me. Do you see how long I have been neglected? Deliver me from the sand and I will crown you king of Upper and Lower Egypt." The Prince got up and gave an order to clear the area surrounding the Sphinx. Shortly thereafter he was crowned King Thutmoses IV. Thutmoses inscribed the dream on the stela and located it between the paws.
>
> Fayed, 29

The New Testament also provides a number of examples of God communicating His Divine Will to individuals through their dreams. For example, the wise men from the east that had prophesied the birth of Jesus from the stars were encouraged by Herod the king of Jerusalem to disclose the location of the child once they had found him. However, after finding the babe and presenting their gifts of gold, frankincense and myrrh, they were "warned of God in a dream that they should not return to Herod, [and] they departed into their own country another way." (Matthew 2:12)

Joseph, the stepfather of Jesus, received a number of Divine communications through his own dreams, including being encouraged to take Mary as his wife in spite of the fact she was already pregnant before their marriage had been conjugated. (Matthew 1:19–24) After the birth of Jesus, Joseph was warned to take his family into Egypt to escape Herod's wrath, and he was also told when it was safe to return. (Matthew 2:13 and 2:20, respectively) When Jesus had grown to adulthood, Pontius Pilate's wife told her husband not to have anything to do with Jesus' crucifixion because Jesus was innocent and she had "suffered many things this day in a dream because of him." (Matthew 27:19)

■

Even today, individuals tell of experiences that they have had suggesting the Divine still can communicate through dreams. In the case of Dave Lawrence, it was the death of his mother-in-law and a dream preceding her death that eventually led to an entirely new understanding of life and his relationship with God. Although the dream was brief and simple, its influence would impact Dave in ways that he could never have imagined.

Raised in a very conservative religious home with a father that preached "the message of a God Who loves us all but was ready to send you to hell for eternity in an instant," Dave did not feel as though he had much of a spiritual upbringing. By the time he was married with a wife and a child, he felt that he lacked any kind of personal direction. Something was missing from his life. By his own account, it was much easier for him to help others with their direction and questions about life than it was for him to help himself. Employed with a customer service company, he had a strong material focus and wanted to get ahead in his career and the organization. In fact, when Dave had his dream experience, his first thought was that it had something to do with the fact that he was going to become financially successful.

Dave admits, "I'm not the kind of person who has psychic experiences, who can feel things beyond the five senses, and I rarely even remember my dreams . . . I'm just a regular guy." However, one morning he remembered a dream that he now believes was of a Divine nature. Even now he feels that it was an answer to his need for personal direction; however, over time, his understanding of what the dream was all about has completely changed:

It was a very short dream. An elderly man, who I knew was some kind of a television actor, was dressed in a very nice suit. He looked very distinguished. He looked me right in the eye and said with a slight but sincere and comforting smile, "The way will be shown to you."

That's all there was to the dream. I awoke feeling elated. I thought my dream was telling me that the way to financial prosperity was going to be shown to me. Little did I know at the time that "the way" was going to be of a spiritual nature.

As time passed and his finances did not improve, Dave became disappointed that the dream had let him down. However, after his mother-in-law died, a couple of events convinced him that his dream had actually been about his own spiritual direction and not his finances. In the first instance, a friend gave him and his wife a book on the Near Death Experience as a means of comforting them after his mother-in-law's passing. For Dave, it became an instrumental turning point in his life and in discovering that there was a God he could truly understand and embrace—a God that was "all loving and forgiving, with no conditions no matter what mistakes we may make. A God that forgives us even before we ask for it."

The second event occurred after Dave had been praying that he would be able to find someone who could help him make progress on his own spiritual path. Shortly thereafter, Dave received a call at work from a woman inquiring about his company's range of services. The two seemed to have an immediate camaraderie, and the conversation extended beyond facts about work to each other's personal interests. The woman discussed her involvement in things of a spiritual nature and mentioned that she belonged to an ecumenical spiritual discussion group. Dave asked if he could visit and she agreed. The group turned out to be a personal godsend, giving Dave a whole new understanding and appreciation of the nature of God. He has been a member of the group ever since.

Although Dave is still working on improving his financial situation, he admits, "It's of less importance than it used to be." Instead, Dave says, "My goal, my life's work, is to become a channel of the Divine. The way has been shown to me and the easiest thing I've ever done is to stay on this path. This is what I really had been looking for!" The dream had not let him down after all.

■

In the case of Linda Owens, a personal crisis involving her daughter's estrangement from the family laid the groundwork for a dream that would provide her with spiritual direction. A registered nurse in her fifties, Linda was distraught when her youngest daughter, then twenty-six, turned away from the family as a means of coping with personal problems. To be cut off from her daughter in such a manner was more than Linda could bear, but regardless of how she tried to reach out, her daughter wanted no further contact between them.

As the estrangement turned to months and then years, Linda's depression worsened. According to Linda, the dream "happened at a time in my life when all I was trying to do on my own was not working and I needed to change my approach." In its essence, the dream suggested that she simply needed to "let go and let God":

In the dream, I was driving up a mountain in a station wagon—alone. Up ahead was my destination, and on the right was a huge sign. However, as I moved up the mountain, the car moved slower and slower. I pushed my foot on the accelerator to the floor but to no avail. The car finally stopped in the middle of the road.

All at once, a man riding a donkey and wearing a white robe appeared next to the car. The man lifted me and the car off the road and pulled it to my destination just as a high-powered car came over the hill ready to crash into me. If it hadn't been for the man in the robe, there would have been an accident.

To Linda, the dream suggested that she needed to rely more on things of a spiritual nature. As a result, she became actively engaged in a spiritual search as a means of coping with the situation. She investigated metaphysics, philosophy, spiritual discussion groups, as well as dream work. To her surprise, in spite of the fact that the situation with her daughter did not change immediately, Linda found that she was better able to deal with it. Both her thoughts and her feelings changed, and although she still loved her daughter, she was able to continue living her own life in spite of the situation.

Thankfully, Linda's daughter did eventually reconcile with the family—a process that took ten years. Today, Linda is involved with energy healing and Healing Touch and continues her work with dreams. She has also learned to honor "each individual's personal beliefs and support his or her own healing, which only can come from within." Even now, she remains convinced that the dream she had about the man in the robe was truly "a personal encounter with the Divine"—one that helped her work through and even flourish during one of the most challenging periods of her life.

■

After a period of his own life challenges, Matt Johnson had a dream that seemed to encourage him to work with personal healing and spirituality. A business manager with a background in marketing, and as a controller, Matt believes that personal problems and a failed marriage led to his Divine encounter: "My anger was so great, my depression was so all-encompassing, my rejection was so deep, I had no where to turn but within." A series of financial setbacks, failed investments and problems with the IRS—all of which had been hidden from his wife—eventually caused a collapse of his home and work life, as well as his emotional well-being. Matt admits that he reached a state of mind in which "I could not take care of myself, let alone a family." He moved out of state as a means of just trying to survive, leaving behind his wife and two grown children.

During this period of what Matt calls "emotional suicide," he began searching for what the next stage of his life should be about. He read books, looked into different branches of philosophy and attended conferences on spirituality. Gradually he began to find answers that seemed to make sense and people who made him feel at home. However, never really "a joiner," Matt kept mostly to himself and continued his independent approach to seeking the answers to life's questions. In the middle of his spiritual investigation, he had a dream that seemed to provide him with a "next step," regarding what he needed to be working on.

In the dream, Matt found himself in the living room with an enormous "high technology machine" that he had just purchased. The machine contained a large video screen that enabled the purchaser to do "remote viewing"—psychically seeing people and events at a distance. Matt states that with the machine he could "see my friends, activities, my family, whatever I wanted." In the dream he could not wait to share this machine with his wife, whom he had divorced in waking life. However, when he showed her the machine, she became very irate that he had made such a purchase without consulting her. It was in the midst of a heated argument that a knock came to their door.

Matt opened the door and found a coach, who was recruiting individuals to play on a basketball team or sports team of some kind. The coach wanted Matt to be one of those players. The next thing Matt remembered was being on the bus, which was being driven around by the coach in order to pick up all of the new recruits. The coach told him that the team would consist of a diverse group of twelve individuals.

After traveling up a hill and witnessing a panoramic view of a beautiful valley, the bus driver/coach was somehow transformed and was wearing a robe and had a beard. In the dream, Matt realized that the coach was Jesus. The bus stopped in front of the home of the twelfth and final recruit:

Jesus was talking to the recruit, who was tiny in stature, skinny, shy and frail looking, at best. Jesus was insisting that the recruit had a part to play and would be a significant participant, no matter what. The recruit, however, insisted that he was too small, too weak, not deserving and probably unable to help.

Jesus, as coach, insisted that diversity was what mattered and that indeed the attributes that the recruit possessed would be used extensively and would balance the team. Everyone had something to contribute . . .

As this conversation was taking place, I looked down at my hands and noticed that three fingers on my right hand were severely deformed. They resembled rotten or blackened overripe bananas. I stuck my hand inside my shirt, knowing that I had a problem. I insisted that I had to HEAL these three fingers before I could play on the team and indeed I would not participate until I did. I had listened to the coach and the newest recruit and decided in order to be a part of this team, I had to heal.

I wanted to play on His team!

Not really understanding what the dream was trying to tell him, Matt acknowledges that the dream "haunted me for a number of months." It was only after continuing his spiritual search, attending a few more conferences, and working with even more dreams that he finally understood what the dream had been all about. The fingers were extensions of himself and his life: "I realized that the three fingers that needed healing represented my ex-wife and my two children. I had been in a state of depression, anger, fear and denial up to that point."

He also remembered that one of the most memorable fights he had with his wife the first year of their marriage was over the purchase of a new color TV set that he had acquired without sharing the decision with her. That memory caused him to realize that the dream was prodding him to work on healing the situation with his family and that his ex-wife could be helpful to him throughout that process. As a result, he and his wife "tried to understand nearly thirty years of life together. For the first time in a long time we began to dialogue in understanding our life's drama."

Matt describes the next seven months of his life as being totally transforming, healing, enlightening, loving and inspirational. He knew that healing his "three fingers" had begun. In the process of healing, he had to encounter his emotions, his tears and his anxieties, but in a very real sense healing took place with his family and he overcame all of his former rage and depression from the past. Although he and his wife did not reconcile as a couple, they did heal the anger from their break-up and have reached a point where they truly understand one another. He has also reconnected with both of his children.

At this point in his life, Matt is eagerly pursuing his life's direction and his career options. He feels that his spiritual search has given him a new understanding of life and a new appreciation for what is truly important. Regardless of where his work next leads him, Matt Johnson has come to understand that no matter what—he wants to be "a significant player on *His* team."

■

It was while Omar Mustaf was still a college student that he had a dream encounter that convinced him not only of the reality of the Divine but also of the numerous ways in which God can interact with humankind. Raised in a traditional Muslim family, Omar—by the time he was a teenager—had begun to seriously question religion as a whole, wondering if many religious traditions and spiritual figures from history were simply human creations. While Omar was attending college, his main courses of study entailed history, science and archaeology. He remembers one day during a History of Religions class when he asked the professor a question that had long been on his mind:

"How do we know that individuals like Moses, Jesus, and Mohammed actually existed? How do we know that these people were not just made up by history and by those that needed to believe?"

Omar recalls that the professor's response did not satisfy his questioning mind at all. The professor pondered the question for a moment and, as Omar remembers, seemed to reply with a series of his own questions:

"Do you know that you have a father?" the professor asked.

"Yes," Omar responded, wondering what that had to do with his question.

"How do you know?"

"Because he has raised me and he continues to be a part of my life."

The professor nodded and asked, "Do you know that you have a grandfather?"

"Yes."

"How do you know?"

"Because he was part of my life before he died."

The professor nodded again and asked, "Did you ever know your great-grandfather?"

"No," Omar shrugged. "He was dead before I was born."

"How do you know that he existed?" The professor inquired.

"Because my father and grandfather both spoke about him and told stories about him."

The professor nodded and stated, "In other words, your great-grandfather was a part of their history, and their memories of him were passed down to their own descendents in order to keep his memory alive."

"Okay."

"In the same way, that's how we know that individuals like Moses, Jesus, and Mohammed really existed. Their contemporaries passed down stories to their own descendents."

Even now Omar recalls that the dialogue with his professor had not been a satisfactory answer to his question. However, that same night Omar remembered a dream that addressed the question he had asked earlier that day:

I remember being all by myself in a familiar setting, like outside of our home. As I was standing there, I suddenly became aware of a powerful presence and a light. When I turned, I was totally surprised because standing behind me were the very three individuals whose existence I had questioned earlier in the day: Moses, Jesus, and Mohammed!

They didn't say anything; the three just looked at me. But I remember their presence was so powerful that I could actually feel it striking against my body like waves of energy. There was no question that I was standing in the presence of three powerful Beings. Even in the dream, I was speechless.

Suddenly, Omar was awakened from the dream and found that even when totally conscious he remained overpowered by what he had just seen. "I was still so overwhelmed that as hard as I tried, I could not speak." The effect lasted several minutes, causing Omar to believe that what he had just seen was much more than a dream: "I have no doubt that I was really in the presence of these three Beings. From that day on, I have never doubted their existence again."

■

In the case of Nancy Abbot, a dream about her deceased boss seemed to be divinely inspired. At the time of the dream, she was facing one of the most challenging periods in her life:

I had been working for ten years as a paralegal for the senior partner and one of the leading litigators of a major law firm in my hometown. I had an excellent work record and had always received the highest rating on my yearly performance appraisals. One day my boss literally dropped dead from a major heart attack. This was a devastating blow because he was a good and decent man and it was the loss not only of a respected boss but of a mentor and father figure, as well.

To make matters worse, her own father's health was in serious decline and he was suffering from various health problems, as well as dementia. Nancy sums up her life at that point by saying, "It was the most difficult and challenging year of my working career."

She recalls how depressed she became after her boss's death. He was a brilliant man, easy to work with and always helpful, greeting each problem with the statement, "Leave it to me and I'll see what I can do." Adding to her personal problems, a number of weeks after her boss's death, Nancy learned that she was going to be laid off by the firm. However, instead of receiving a cash severance for her release, she was given a "working severance," which meant that she was going to have to continue working up until her last day—receiving payment for her work but nothing beyond her last date of employment. Understandably, she was devastated.

As part of Nancy's own spiritual path at the time, she had been regularly saying a portion of Psalm 51 each day and sometimes several times through the day: "Create in me a pure heart, O Lord and . . . sustain me with Your bountiful spirit." Nancy continued using the psalm as a personal affirmation whenever her problems seemed overwhelming. She found that she had to use the affirmation repeatedly:

It is not pleasant to have to go into work every day and face people who have decided that they don't want you anymore. I was angry and hurt at the way I had been treated, and I knew that my deceased boss would have been upset by this turn of events. I continued to go to work and tried to maintain the same level of competence as before, mainly for the sake of the clients, but for my own personal integrity, as well.

It wasn't until Nancy had a dream about her boss that she started to feel better about her personal situation:

In the dream, I was in an office building. I passed the door of an office and saw my deceased boss sitting behind the desk. I was delighted to see him (this was the first time I had dreamed about him since he died), and I went in eagerly to say hello and to ask how he was.

We talked for a bit (I can't remember what about), and then as I was going to get up to go, he said that he knew something was bothering me and wondered if I wanted to talk about it. I didn't want to bother him, but I sat back down and told him what had happened at work after he had died. He said that he was aware of what had gone on and was very disappointed in his partners because he did not believe I deserved to be treated in that way. He then said, "Leave it with me and I'll see what I can do."

Her meeting with her boss and his familiar statement gave her a great deal of comfort. For some reason, it gave her the feeling that somehow things would work out in the end. However, her last day came and went without fanfare. Suddenly, she was out of work and out of severance. For six weeks, Nancy was without a job. Perhaps surprisingly, Nancy felt that the time off turned out to be a blessing. Her father's health continued to decline, and the layoff enabled her to spend much time with him during his final days.

A couple of weeks after her father's death, Nancy received a phone call from the law firm for which she had been working. The company wanted her to come back! As it turned out, her return proved to be even more financially beneficial than if she had never been laid off in the first place. Nancy states happily, "I was called back to work six weeks after I had been laid off, and I was able to negotiate an even better contract because they needed my services so badly." Rather than facing unemployment and financial hardship, Nancy's experience had been a blessing in disguise. Just as she frequently requested in her daily affirmation, throughout it all the bountiful spirit of the Divine had sustained her. She also has no doubt that somehow her boss had kept his word and intervened on her behalf.

■

In another instance, the horror of World War II and the resulting memories caused Christine Martin to sink into a state of emotional depression. By the time she was nineteen, her brother and many classmates that she had gone through years of school with had been killed in the war. Her brother had been only twenty-four at the time of his death, and Christine was devastated by the loss. However, Christine suppressed her feelings and went on with her life.

Five years passed, and when Christine turned twenty-four, she married a wonderful husband. The war was over, and she knew that she should be happy with her life; however, the realization that she was now the same age that her brother had been when he was killed caused her to sink to a new emotional low:

I was so totally clogged up with "war memories," not just my own personal experiences but thoughts of what had happened all over the world. My life seemed to have no meaning or direction. I just wanted out of the misery I was living in. I tearfully prayed and cried out for God to "Take me!" I was so young . . . but it would have been okay if I simply died.

Shortly thereafter, Christine had a dream. In the dream, she was sleeping in her own bed and saw the "robe of Jesus" just above her head. She reached up to grab the hem of the robe, believing that if she could catch onto the garment, she would be taken with Him:

I was crying, tears tolling down my face, and begging Jesus to "Take me!" His robe stayed just barely out of my reach, like an inch away from my outstretched fingers. I was begging and reaching with all of my might and strength to try and grasp the robe.

All of a sudden, I heard the voice of Jesus say, "No, not yet." The voice was a voice of love, filled with so much love that I was immediately satisfied in my soul.

When Christine awoke, her face was still covered with tears. She became conscious of the darkness of her room and realized that in the dream she had been surrounded by immense Light. She also knew that somehow she had been in the presence of Christ. Her heart seemed filled with the love she had felt during the dream, and Christine became aware of the fact that both her depression and her feelings of wanting to die had suddenly vanished. Somehow she had been healed in a dream by a Divine encounter.

Today, Christine is eighty years old but still recalls the dream with as much clarity as if it occurred yesterday. "It felt so peaceful . . . it was an answer to my prayer to be taken, and it did 'take me' in consciousness to something beyond anything I had ever imagined." Even now Christine is convinced that Love lifted her out of her depression and left her with a lesson that is still relevant in her heart today: "Love life, love others, love myself, love the Lord thy God with all thy heart, mind and soul." With that in mind, Christine adds, "Life is so simple."

■

The story of Wilma Jenkins' life contains an incredibly varied religious background, as well as a depth of depression that took her years to overcome. Stating that she has always been a seeker, Wilma describes her religious path as follows: "I was raised as a Lutheran, became a Baptist and a born-again Christian in high school, left that and became reformed Jewish during college, left that and became a Catholic during my marriage." She has been practicing Catholicism for the past thirty years but is also deeply interested in metaphysics, meditation—which she now calls "the core" of her spiritual life—and personal guidance from her dreams.

Wilma believes that her emotional problems as a young woman were originally brought on by post-partum depression. While in the depths of her depression, she attempted suicide and was in a coma for four days. She eventually recovered and decided not to kill herself, but even then the depression remained with her:

> My greatest personal struggle is depression. Even after the threat of suicide was no longer an issue, it was hard for me to get up and go to work. I used to pray as I walked to the subway for a "lightness of mood" so that I wouldn't burden my coworkers.

To be sure, at the time, her depression was having a major impact on her relationship with her husband. Wilma recalls one night when they had an intense argument in which "he was obviously very wrong." That night she had a dream:

I was in the bathroom in my apartment building. Suddenly, the ceiling above me broke open and a toilet fell through, almost landing on my head. Through the hole in the ceiling, I saw my husband in the room above. I was furious, as it was obvious to me that he had had another temper tantrum and could not control his anger, hurling the toilet through the floor. I complained loudly and bitterly about this.

Suddenly, a little old man with a gray beard appeared and said to me, "The fault lies in *your* ideas, because obviously the toilet could not have broken through a sound floor. Your ceiling is defective."

Even upon awaking, Wilma realized that she had just been taught a very important lesson; part of the problem had to do with her the "ceiling" in her mind: her own thought-processes and her attitude. Much later, she had another dream in which she asked to be healed:

In the dream, I was praying with a television evangelist as he was doing healing prayer for various people who had written him. All at once, I heard a voice that said, "What do you want?" The voice came from the upper right corner of the room and sounded very serious.

While still dreaming, Wilma realized that the voice was the voice of the archangel Michael. Rather than being a comforting angelic presence, he emanated sternness. Even his voice sounded very serious. Gathering her bravery, Wilma managed to stutter, "I think I would like to heal." The dream ended and she awoke.

These dreams and others prompted Wilma to place even greater emphasis on her own spiritual search. She began to meditate. She learned that regardless of how badly she felt or how she sensed she had failed, "it is most important to get up and try again." Her dreams encouraged her not to lose hope even in the midst of her depression. She began working with spiritual disciplines and using personal affirmations to help bolster her mood. As if in answer to her request, she noticed that things eventually started to change:

Once I began having personal guidance experiences, the reality of the closeness of God and the enormity of our responsibility as souls became a part of me. I no longer felt that God was "up there" while we were down here. I began to understand how we can love those who hurt us; I began to understand the meaning of God's unconditional love. I did it by persevering with application of spiritual disciplines on all levels: body, mind and soul.

No longer bothered by the depression that plagued her, Wilma has grown immensely over the years. Now a widow and mother of two grown children, she says that she has learned that she is truly a child of God and as such had no right to loathe herself for such a long time. In terms of why she had the personal experiences that prompted her to begin healing her depression, she says simply, "When our consciousness is in the mud, that's when we need to be lifted the most."

■

Even though she was only eighteen years old at the time, Eileen Smith was certain that the two things she wanted most in life would forever be beyond her reach. Calling them "major disappointments," Eileen was devastated when her father's crop failures on the family farm forced her to postpone her college plans indefinitely. To make matters worse, the young man she had fallen in love with was moving away to West Point for his own college plans: "He was so caught up in his own future that he was not that interested in me. He was moving away, and I was convinced that I could never fall for anyone else."

The issues of her departing boyfriend and her failed college plans had prompted her to become depressed, frustrated and uncertain about facing a future in which everything that seemed important to her was somehow spinning out of control. She found herself becoming negative and overwhelmed by the helplessness of her situation. However, there didn't seem to be anything that she could do, nor was there any way to change what was happening. The love of her life was leaving, and her own college plans were over.

Perhaps Eileen's saving grace at the time was her interest in religion. Although her family was "not particularly interested in religion," Eileen's desire to go to church often prompted her mother and sister to follow along. On one such occasion while she was still dealing with the helplessness of her situation, the three women attended church together. Eileen remembers that during the service the minister gave an impassioned call for members of the congregation to come forward and accept Christ into their hearts. Caught up in the moment, Eileen followed much of the congregation down to the front of the church. The day was memorable mostly because it seemed to facilitate a dream that she had shortly thereafter:

I dreamed that I was in a moonlit garden, standing at a gate. It was very beautiful. Two awesome angels appeared to me. They were very large, had full wings and were dressed in angelic regalia. They asked me if I would like to be baptized. I answered yes, somewhat fearfully. (I don't think I would have dared say no!)

They led me to a round pool. It seemed like a pool and a deep well at the same time. They told me to step into the pool. I protested, saying that I didn't really know how to swim and was afraid that I might drown. They insisted and assured me that they would be watching me.

As I got into the water, it was very deep. It started spinning like a whirlpool. I started fighting to stay up and was reaching for help. I was being drawn deeper and deeper into the whirlpool. I looked up and saw the two angels just watching me but making no attempt to help me at all. I fought and fought, sinking deeper and deeper. I finally gave up, knowing that I was going to die. I looked up one more time and saw Jesus.

He leaned down and extended his right hand, and I reached up with my right hand. Instantly, I was out of the water. I remember sitting beside him on a rocky ledge and talking with him, but I don't remember what he told me.

When Eileen awoke the next day, she felt instantly relieved of her disappointments. The hopelessness that she had felt was gone: "I went around in a glow for weeks." At the same time, however, not knowing really what the dream meant, Eileen was needlessly concerned that it suggested some kind of a calling to be a missionary, "and I wanted no part of that."

Today, however, looking back on the dream, she can see that although her life at the time felt as though it were "spinning out of control," she really had nothing to worry about. In spite of her fears, she did marry someone else and have two children. During her marriage, she also went on to college and earned her degree. Her dream occurred just when she needed comforting the most and was apparently an attempt to reassure her that the Divine would reach out and support her even when things seemed as though they were hopeless. The experience was also the first in a series that have helped her understand one of her most meaningful life lessons. That lesson has been the importance of refocusing her thoughts from dwelling on what she does not want to happen, to thinking instead about what she really does want.

■

It was a dream about Jesus that also helped inspire Robert Clayton to follow through on his desire to be of service and to get on with a task that needed to be done. Recently elected to the board of an ecumenical spiritual organization, Robert was uncertain about his role as a new board member. The night before his first meeting, a dream set the tone for what would become his own life's direction and focus. He dreamed that he was in a hotel lobby not far from where the board meeting was taking place:

I'm in the lobby, and it's very, very bright—almost to the point of hurting your eyes. I'm talking to a group of people and telling them, "He's coming; He's coming." The people do not listen but instead turn their backs on me and walk away to the back of the lobby.

Suddenly, through a revolving door, in walks the Master dressed in a western suit. There are others with him. As he comes toward me, I automatically go to my knees and have a feeling that I haven't done enough of what I'm supposed to do. I feel very sad and depressed. Jesus would have none of that, and he raised me up from my knees. I heard his voice, but there were no words spoken—only thoughts back and forth.

"It's been since Palestine since we've seen each other." I remember that there was absolutely no condemnation from Him or about Him—He made me feel happiness!

As He brought me completely to my feet, the thought came, "Robert, you know what you have to do—I'm going to help these people who won't listen."

The dream inspired Robert and enabled him to instill that enthusiasm in other members of the board. He realized that even as a new board member, he had an important role to play. In time, he became known as "a Jesus person," one who consistently reached out to others, regardless of their religious beliefs or affiliation. The reference to Palestine also proved interesting because Robert holds a strong belief in the reality of reincarnation and in his own previous experiences at the time of Jesus.

■

Finally, in the case of Mary Phillips, a dream helped her to understand how the Divine works to bring together individuals who are important to one another. Raised by a foster family, Mary's birth mother, Adele, gave her up at birth. It wasn't until years later that Mary reconnected with her biological mother and the woman became a close part of Mary's life and family. According to Mary, "My four children adored her, and she was very fond of them."

Adele was apparently fondest of Mary's youngest son, Terry, and loved it when he and Mary would come to see her. After one visit when Terry was eleven, Adele wrote the boy and told him that she had dreamed that Terry was her son—a dream that simply illustrated how much she loved the boy. That same year, Mary and Terry were both with Adele when she died.

Years passed, and Terry had grown and married, and he and his wife were expecting their first child. During the final month of pregnancy, Mary had a dream about her birth mother that seemed especially lucid:

In the dream, I was with my biological mother, and she was wearing the gown I had purchased for her a few months before she died. She did not appear ill in the dream. The time came to say goodbye, and I went to her and put my arms around her and said, "Adele, I have to go now."

She looked at me with a strange look and said, "But Honey, today is my birthday!"

For a moment I felt terrible, thinking that I hadn't even bought her a birthday card. I abruptly awoke still worried about it.

Suddenly, Mary realized that her mother had been dead for years and that the woman's birth date had been in May, not August 31st, which was the day it was. The dream was puzzling, and Mary told it to a friend later in the day.

That evening, Terry called to say that his wife had given birth to a daughter, whom they called Barbara. The dream made Mary wonder about the connection between her birth mother and her new granddaughter; however, Mary did not say anything about the dream to her granddaughter for ten years.

As time passed, however, Mary began to notice amazing similarities between Barbara and Adele. Those similarities included both personality traits and talents: Barbara was a very extraverted little girl; Adele was extremely extraverted herself. Adele loved singing and even sang professionally; Barbara has a beautiful singing voice, as well. Over the years, Mary found herself studying Barbara to see the similarities between the child and Adele. There proved to be similarities in actions, personality traits, manners of expression and even likes and dislikes. The dream and these similarities, plus Adele's own fondness for Terry, who is Barbara's father, have caused Mary to believe that her mother has reincarnated as her grandchild. When Barbara was ten, Mary decided to tell about the dream. Barbara accepted it all matter-of-factly.

The whole experience has convinced Mary of the reality of reincarnation and the fact that we are brought back together with those we love for a continuation of life's lessons and our own personal development. To her it is simply a Divine insight that was confirmed by a dream.

4

Life's Challenges and the Presence of the Divine

This pure mind, the source of everything, shines on all with the brilliance of its own perfection, but the people of the world do not awake to it . . . Because their understanding is veiled by their own site, hearing, feeling, and knowledge, they do not perceive the spiritual brilliance of the original substance. If they could only eliminate all analytical thinking in a flash, that original substance would manifest itself like the sun ascending through the void and illuminating the whole universe without hindrance or bounds.

Teachings of the
Compassionate Buddha, 197

One of the most unique accounts of experiencing the Divine presence after having gone through a series of life's challenges is the story of Irina Tweedie and her spiritual liberation through the teachings of a Sufi master. Irina would become the first Western woman trained in the ancient lineage of Naqshbandi Sufism—a mystical branch of Islam known as the Silent Sufis. A diary of her experiences under her guru's tutelage would grow to become the classic *The Chasm of Fire,* selling more than 100,000 copies and eventually being translated into six languages. The book's popularity would cause her to include even more excerpts from her diary in an expanded 800-page version entitled *Daughter of Fire,* which also became a best-seller.

Irina Tweedie's life spanned a variety of cultures, personal experiences and spiritual searches. She was born in Russia in 1907 and would eventually be educated in both Vienna and Paris. She moved to England in the 1930s and would become the wife of a British banker. Her first husband died during World War II. After the war, she met and married an English naval officer, with whom she fell deeply in love. When her second husband died as a relatively young man, she became so depressed that she no longer wanted to live. However, his death inspired her to begin a spiritual search that would forever transform her life. An avid reader, she discovered a book on the subject of reincarnation, which introduced her to Theosophy. She joined the Theosophical Society, devoured many books on the immortality of the soul and was eventually inspired to move to India in 1961 at the age of fifty-four in search of a spiritual guru. Her search led her to a Sufi master and teacher who encouraged her to keep a spiritual journal of her experiences.

When she first encountered her Sufi master, she explained that she had come to India in search of God. "I want God," she told him, "but not the Christian idea of an anthropomorphic deity sitting somewhere, possibly on a cloud surrounded by angels with harps; I want the Rootless Root, the Causeless Cause of the Upanishads." (Tweedie, *Daughter*, 8) Mrs. Tweedie might never have imagined what her personal search for God would entail.

Her Sufi master's approach for her spiritual training seemed to be one in which her personality was ground down through hardship and challenge. Her spiritual "training" would entail the process of abandoning the little self of the ego and removing the veils of her personality so that she could uncover the inner truth within herself and ultimately reach the level of her soul. Mrs. Tweedie's experiences suggest that during moments of great desperation, when the individual feels totally helpless and abandoned, at those moments true clarity and spiritual illumination can often take place. Her teacher had told her, "Keep a diary. One day it will become a book. But you must write it in such a way that it should help others . . . " (Tweedie, *Chasm*, 7) According to Mrs. Tweedie, she wondered if others would understand:

When I was writing my book, *Daughter of Fire,* how often did I wonder how many people would understand what it was all about, why did I do it, why did I strive and suffer and fight with myself? Who would understand the burning desire to be able to touch the outermost edges of conscious awareness where, I dimly felt, must be hidden the secret which leads to absolute freedom? Freedom from the bondage which chains us to the wheel of life . . .

The taming of the ego is a painful process. It is a crucifixion. One does not lose anything, or get rid of anything. "You cannot become anything else but what you already are," said Carl Jung. We just learn to control our lower self and it becomes our servant, not our master. The master is the Real Us, our soul, and the real wisdom is in the soul. (Vaughan-Lee, xii)

The process of her spiritual liberation proved to be a painful one. She was forced to undergo loneliness, depression, humiliation, overwhelming heat and the challenge of having to face all of the imperfections within herself. On occasion she encountered horrible hallucinations that seemed to originate from the recesses of her mind. More than once she described herself as being filled with terror and convinced that she was going mad with fear. At times, Irina described her state of mind as being one of absolute despair, even causing her to contemplate suicide on a couple of occasions:

> It is a peculiar, special feeling of utter loneliness . . . All seems dark and lifeless. There is no purpose anywhere or in anything. No God to pray to. No hope. Nothing at all . . .
>
> The nights are still, full of stars and oven-hot. A sheer agony. My eyes are constantly red and inflamed from the perspiration running into them. Men go around with twisted handkerchiefs around their foreheads to prevent this happening, and some wear twisted towels around their necks. I shower three to four times a day but there is no relief as the water tank is on the roof and the water is boiling hot.
>
> . . . the temperature yesterday was 117° in the shade. Today it felt even hotter, like the entrance hall of hell . . .
>
> Tweedie, Chasm, 100–101

> The nights are a potential nightmare. I dread to go home every

evening. Lying still for hours trying to control this body of mine, shaken by forces almost too powerful to be controlled. In the morning I am shaky, my knees give way, can hardly walk; there is a strong feeling of nausea. I eat very little and often wonder how it is that all the other functions of the body go on seemingly normally. Tweedie, Chasm, 61–62

So much sorrow is in me that there is no speech left to express it . . . my body is defeating me because of the vomiting condition, and I can hardly eat. I also have reasons to think that my eyesight is deteriorating because I am weeping so much.

Tweedie, Chasm, 86

Mrs. Tweedie's experiences of personal suffering, resulting from a combination of heat, noise, depression, physical illness and emotional distress, eventually resulted in an emptying of her personality. Later, she would recall:

I had hoped to get instructions in Yoga, expected wonderful teachings, but what the Teacher did was mainly to force me to face the darkness within myself, and it almost killed me . . . I was beaten down in every sense till I had to come to terms with that in me which I kept rejecting all my life. Tweedie, Daughter, x

Eventually her training and her personal surrender proved worthwhile, for Irina discovered a depth of the presence of love that she had never known existed. Sufi tradition states that "God is Love," and according to Sufi beliefs, that same truth is ultimately applicable to every human being because all of humankind are children of the Divine who have been "made in His Image." According to Irina, "in our innermost being, in the very core of ourselves, we will find a place where there is peace, stillness and, above all, love." Tweedie, Daughter, 821

Our relationship to God is something entirely different from what we usually imagine it to be. We think that the relationship of

> God and man is of duality. There is God and there is the man who will pray to God asking for something, or who will worship, or love, or praise God. There are always two. But it is not so. I have found that our relationship to God is something quite different. It is a merging, without words, without thought even . . . into something. Something so tremendous, so endless, merging in infinite love . . . Tweedie, Daughter, 631

Irina came to understand and to personally experience the presence of God. She also gained an awareness of each individual's contribution to the Whole, which she described as "The Realization that every act, every word, every thought of ours not only influences our environment but for some mysterious reason forms an integral and important part of the Universe . . . ." (Tweedie, *Daughter,* 812) Her hardships had enabled her to find what she had been looking for in a way that she had never expected. Irina came to experience the truth of "God is love," becoming a master of the Sufi tradition in her own right.

After her guru's death in 1966, she returned to London. When she was asked what it was like being with a Sufi master for five years, she often replied, "It was like being run over by a steamroller." (Vaughan-Lee, 132) After her transformative experience, she lectured throughout England, Europe and the United States and led meditation meetings and classes in her home. She taught others about the Sufi tradition she had finally mastered. She came to know the all-pervading Presence of the Divine that resides just beyond the awareness of most individuals. From her perspective, it is a Presence that can become accessible to anyone who surrenders his or her personality self through choice, through hardship or through desperation. After lecturing and teaching for many years, Irina finally retired in 1991. She died in England in 1999. Her work continues through the Golden Sufi Center in Inverness, California.

■

Similar to what Irina Tweedie experienced by choice, Lori Upton encountered through a combination of life's events. Like Irina, Lori's experience suggests that oftentimes when an individual has nowhere else to turn, it is often in that state of mind that he or she becomes aware of the presence of God.

Today Lori Upton is a fifty-year-old woman with three grown children. Her personal encounter with the Divine occurred about seven years ago when she felt completely beaten down by family problems and was suffering from severe depression and recurring migraines. To make matters worse, during her depression it seemed as if she had also become sensitized to the day-to-day problems in the world: violence, hatred, negativity—all of the news she saw in the newspapers and on television often caused her to feel overwhelmed. Her job was also a challenge, as she had undergone a career setback because of changes at her company. Everything about her life seemed out of control, and there was nothing she could do to fix it. Summing up her overall situation, Lori says simply:

> My sons were experimenting with hard drugs, getting into trouble and generally failing at having productive lives. My daughter was depressed and failing in school. My marriage was adversely affected because of what was happening with the children, and communication between my husband and me was practically non-existent. I dreaded going to work. I dreaded getting up in the morning. Everything about my life was completely out of control, and I felt very much alone and unsupported.

Her depression only worsened when she thought about the family problems that had affected her throughout her life. Because her mother had been unable to care for her as a child, Lori had been in and out of foster homes for the first six years of her life. Although she was reconciled with her mother at the age of seven, both her parents were alcoholics, and her mother was mentally ill—diagnosed with paranoid schizophrenia. When Lori was thirteen, her mother left the family once and for all. This background made her feel only worse about her situation. There were many times when she told herself, "Wouldn't it be better if I could just die?"

One night Lori felt that she had come to the end of her sanity. To calm herself, she tried to meditate without success. She also tried to pray but found it almost impossible: "There were no words to express the depth of grief that I felt." She felt that she was at her wit's end and had nowhere else to turn—she wanted to scream out loud. Instead, she remembers falling to her knees, feeling her grief well up within her. She remembers wondering to herself if God could hear her scream because He didn't seem to be able to hear her prayers. Suddenly, right before her eyes, she saw a brilliant flash of light:

> The flash of light caught my attention and momentarily snapped me out of my self-pity. All at once, I heard a gentle, compassionate voice ask, "Tell me now what is so terrible? I AM LISTENING."

According to Lori, "I knew I was in the Presence of something holy." Following the voice's request, she began to describe everything that was wrong with her life. She talked about her depression, her family problems, and her feelings of being overwhelmed. She had intended to speak aloud about everything that had been on her mind, but "halfway through my barrage an incredible peace fell over me, and I became quiet." While still aware of the Presence, she suddenly realized that she was not the only one in the world with problems—everyone has something that they have to deal with:

> I was ashamed and embarrassed for having been so into self-pity. Everyone on earth has something difficult to bear. That's why we're here: simply to do our best, to learn and to love.

With the realization that she was not alone in her problems, Lori felt overcome with light. The light filled her with the awareness that she was loved and that each individual was watched over by the Presence of the Divine:

> It was a feeling of awe—a realization that God knows me as an individual, that God knows my pain, knows everything that is in my heart. But it wasn't only this knowledge that was and remains so comforting; it was the knowledge that this love and compassion is shared with every individual: my sons, my daughter, my husband, everyone every-

where! I suddenly realized that we are never really alone. God knows us all. The experience made me feel connected with every other soul . . . I was truly blessed with a moment of grace.

Although her experience with the Divine Presence lasted only a short time, its influence has endured. Even now, Lori can recall her experience and admits that the awareness of this ever-present nature of God has never left her:

The experience has helped me to realize that God is aware of everything, of all of us. It has given me the awareness that He/She knows us each by name and has never given up on any of us. It also helped me to understand that with hope and faith, eventually everything will work out just fine. I have learned not to give up on others or myself . . . patience, compassion and understanding have all become very much a part of my being.

According to Lori, it was an encounter that forever changed her inner being and gave her the determination to "keep on keeping on."

■

Similarly, Keith Reynolds had the experience of being overwhelmed by life's events and having nowhere else to turn. His challenges were personal, professional and financial. In terms of his marriage, neither he nor his wife was happy. For several years they had discussed getting a divorce, but the couple had overextended themselves financially, with numerous bills and an enormous house payment, and there did not appear to be any way out of the situation. The couple had been together for ten years. He was also terrified of being by himself: "even a bad marriage seemed better than being alone."

In terms of his job, Keith had been an executive at his company for more than a dozen years in a job he did well but had become "totally burned out in." He had made haphazard attempts to find a more creative position, but no other company had been willing to match the salary level he required. His job underwent a serious threat when the company's board surprised everyone by calling an emergency meeting and unexpectedly removing Keith's boss, the CEO. The CEO was immediately replaced with an individual from outside the company—someone who knew little about the company, its employees, its culture and its history. According to Keith, "the new CEO was a complete unknown." All at once, rumors begin that the new president was going to remove all of the existing executives and substitute his own executive team in their place.

As Keith's stress from work increased, his marriage became even more challenging. He began to drink every night "just to calm my nerves." Unfortunately, the more he drank, the more he argued with his wife and the more anxious his problems seemed to become. Every time his new boss called him to a meeting, he wondered whether or not he was about to be fired. Part of him just wanted to get in the car and start driving away, but he was crippled by a mountain of debt and the fact that he didn't know where he could go or what he might do.

His ongoing arguments with his wife finally caused her to insist that they follow through on their breakup and put the house up for sale. Keith was worried because the housing market was in a slump and he feared that they would not even be able to recoup the amount of their mortgage: "Even if we sold the house, I would have even more debt to deal with." Nonetheless, the house was put on the market, and he and his wife moved into separate bedrooms. The prospect of all that was to come made him feel worse. He drank even more and kept a bottle in his bedroom so that his wife wouldn't know how far down he had gone. Finally, Keith remembers realizing that he did not have the physical or emotional stamina to take the stress any longer:

> I remember telling a good friend that I was just giving up. I didn't care what happened to me because I couldn't worry about it any more. I was making myself sick, and there was nothing I could do to fix anything. I even told my wife: "I GIVE UP!" Although not a particularly religious person, I remember driving into work that same day and telling God, "You deal with all of this because I can't. Whatever happens is fine. I just can't worry about it anymore."

Almost immediately, Keith felt as if a tremendous weight had been lifted off his shoulders. Even though nothing had changed, he suddenly felt very different. It was as if some kind of light had entered his body and all of his troubles suddenly seemed lighter. He didn't feel the need to worry. He no longer felt the need to drink to calm his nerves. A few days later, when his good friend asked him how things were going, Keith remembers thinking about it for a few moments and then replying with honesty, "You know, I haven't had a bad five minutes since we last talked!" That realization caught him by surprise. Keith remembers thinking about it every day after that for the next few weeks:

> Even though nothing had really changed, my whole attitude had changed. When I tried to discover what was different within me, I remember thinking how I felt more compassion than I had ever felt before. Rather than worrying about *my* job, I was more concerned with whether or not my new boss had all the information he needed in order to make informed decisions about the company. All at once, I was more concerned about my wife's financial situation after our divorce than I was about my own. Whenever one of my employees had a problem, I remember feeling compassion for the individual first and then trying to figure out how I could work with the employee so that we could solve the problem together . . . It may sound funny, but one day I remember thinking to myself that it felt like I had a part of God's love inside of me and I was suddenly able to share that love with others.

A few weeks passed, and when his good friend asked if he was still doing well, Keith answered, "You're going to think I'm crazy, but I still haven't had a bad five minutes." More than that, Keith realized that he hadn't even had "one bad thought about any individual the entire time." I didn't tell my friend, but I thought to myself, "This must be what grace is all about."

To his surprise, the next thing that happened was his house sold for more money than it had been appraised for to a couple that wanted to close and move in immediately. Even after paying closing costs, the realtor and paying off the old mortgage, Keith and his wife were left with $20,000. Keith was totally surprised because he had thought they would be approximately $20,000 to $30,000 in the hole. Because the money was unexpected, Keith gave it to his soon-to-be ex-wife, "just because it seemed like the fair thing to do." The couple continued the divorce proceedings, remaining amicable with one another throughout the entire process. Since that time, his ex-wife has moved out of state, but the two still speak on occasion by phone and remain on friendly terms with one another.

After the house closing had settled and about five weeks after the new company president had started, Keith was called to the CEO's office and given some new responsibilities: "I was really excited because it made my job much more creative." In addition, the boss surprised Keith by giving him a 28% raise! "I was floored . . . I had never gotten a raise like that in my entire life!" Because Keith had told his friend twice previously that "I haven't had a bad five minutes," it became a topic of frequent conversation between them: "I told him that I didn't understand how it was possible, but everything was still unbelievably perfect. It was like I had somehow gotten into the flow of the universe and nothing seemed to interrupt that flow. It was truly a remarkable experience!"

About six months after his wife moved out of state, Keith met another woman, and within a couple of years the two had married. Everything that Keith had once been worried about was somehow miraculously solved. Looking back on that period of his life, Keith describes it this way:

> I know my experience may not sound that incredible to some people, but it was truly incredible for me. It lasted for about six weeks. Imagine having six weeks without thinking one bad thought about anyone; six weeks without worrying about anything; six weeks of being in a great mood and feeling a depth of love inside your heart for other people. It was the most amazing six weeks of my life. I know that it was six weeks of being touched by God.

■

Another example of a Divine encounter occurring in the midst of personal hardship is the case of Lorraine Garner. Today, Lorraine is a forty-seven-year-old woman, but she can still recall her Divine encounter at the age of eleven with as much clarity as on the day it occurred. That experience enabled her to survive a lifetime of challenges and gain an understanding that there is much more to each individual than simply a physical body.

The most traumatic experience of Lorraine's life occurred when she was nine years old and her mother died. She and her ten-year-old sister were left in the care of her father—a man who was unable to reassure either one of them or give them comfort. In fact, her father's own grief caused him to say on many occasions, "Your mother would not have died if she hadn't have had you," attributing the woman's death to the birth of a second child. Although her mother's death had been due to uterine cancer, Lorraine accepted her father's pronouncement and tried hard to understand what she had done to kill her mother. In time, her depression led to fear. Her childish mind began to imagine that the only recompense for having committed such a crime would be to die, as well. At night she often waited in fear for the time when God would hand out her punishment. She stopped sleeping regularly. She became anxious and depressed. She felt alone and overwhelmed. Finally, at the age of eleven, she had a nervous breakdown. According to Lorraine, "I have very little recollection regarding that time period of my life." Apparently the family dealt with the situation as best as they could.

Later that year, when Lorraine, her sister, her father and her grandmother were visiting St. Joseph's Cathedral in Montreal, Canada, Lorraine had a Divine encounter that prompted a healing. She remembers that her family was sitting in one of the pews and the organ was playing near the altar at the front of the church. She was listening to the most beautiful music she had ever heard when suddenly she felt as though something lifted her up and raised her out of her seat. Without explanation, she felt moved to walk toward the altar. As she started walking toward the music, she heard her sister say, "Dad, look at Lorraine!"

As she walked, Lorraine felt as though she were walking on clouds: "It felt like cotton candy was under my feet. It was an incredible sensation." As she walked toward the altar, it seemed as if the sun had somehow entered her body: "I felt like I should be burning up because of the intensity of the light, but I was filled with the most wonderful warmth."

All at once she became aware of the presence of Jesus and her mother, both walking at her side:

> They told me that I was going to have a tough life but that I would be okay . . . During that walk, I felt such love like I have never known before. I knew that communication was happening, but it was hard to explain because it was coming from a place that I did not understand at the time. When I finally reached the altar, I just stood there for a few minutes . . . Tears were coming down my face, but I wasn't conscious of crying.

Later, when Lorraine's sister asked her what had happened, she said simply, "Jesus and Mommy just walked and talked with me." After the experience, the eleven-year-old felt healed of her breakdown. She was no longer afraid. She no longer felt at fault for the death of her mother. She felt like a normal eleven-year-old girl. However, true to the prediction that she received, Lorraine has had a challenging life.

When she was fourteen, she was diagnosed with severe juvenile diabetes and was hospitalized. Because her condition was hard for her father to witness, he never came to see her during her confinement and treatment. The next year, when she was fifteen, a member of her family's church raped her. She survived the experience and married at nineteen. During her first pregnancy, she suffered two bouts of mononucleosis and was forced to have a therapeutic abortion that left her devastated, especially when she learned that the aborted fetus had been twins. After five years of marriage, her husband divorced her. In order to survive and support herself, Lorraine was forced to work several jobs at a time, even having to baby-sit in exchange for food. During these experiences, Lorraine taught herself to stop asking "Why?" Instead, she recalled her encounter, asked for Divine guidance and found the inner strength and the determination to continue on. In a very real sense, her childhood encounter enabled her to deal with the rest of life's challenging events.

A survivor, today Lorraine describes her philosophy as follows:

> I don't fear death. I understand that there is much more to our makeup than a body. I try not to worry or have the need to control

situations. I try not to blame people for the things that life brings my way. I feel there is always a reason—not as a punishment but as a lesson. In the past, I had a hard time being alone; now it doesn't bother me. I stopped looking to others to tell me how to act or what to believe. I trust myself, and I expect much from myself.

Thirteen years after her divorce, Lorraine remarried. Her second husband is someone who shares her beliefs and her philosophy. Her only regret is that she wishes she had been older when her encounter occurred so that she would have more fully understood the experience—an experience that would impact her for the rest of her life. However, she admits, "As I look back, I know it truly enabled me to realize that there is always a reason for what happens to us and, just as I had been reassured, I would always be okay."

■

Gail Beckman is an educated woman with a master's degree in education. A former schoolteacher, Gail is convinced that God gave her a humorous sign as encouragement to follow through on healing an estranged relationship. She understands that many individuals would see her experience as simply her imagination, but she cautions that it actually prompted her to continue a spiritual search that is still very important to her.

A major disagreement with a friend had led to a break-up of their once-close friendship. Gail wanted to call and make amends, but she lacked the bravery to simply follow through. According to Gail, repeatedly the problem "kept eating at me," but she kept ignoring her feelings. Finally, one day when she was at home by herself with the television on, she prayed fervently for guidance as to what she should do and asked God to give her a sign "on the very next commercial on TV, whether or not I should call." Gail tells the story:

God must have a sense of humor because the very next commercial was for Viagra, and the theme song being played was "I'm ready! Ready as a body can be." I was truly impressed and even smiled, but the ad that followed even put icing on the cake. I can't even remember what the commercial was for, but the theme song was "Love is in the air . . . Love is all around." I have never heard that second commercial since. However, I felt like I had been answered. These two commercials gave me the encouragement to pick up the phone and dial.

Still somewhat hesitant, Gail states that she immediately found comfort: "It felt almost like an arm was around my shoulder. It gave me the strength to learn to trust and act on my feelings." When her friend finally answered, the conversation went much better than Gail had anticipated—things could have been much worse. Gail ended the conversation by suggesting that they could continue to work on healing their relationship.

Although her friendship has yet to return to its former closeness, she still considers the whole experience a "successful step in my spiritual growth." She is convinced that the message she received came in direct response to her request and proved to be just a tiny example of the ongoing presence of a "trusting, accepting, kind and all-loving God."

■

Dr. Wendy Preston experienced a number of hardships with her husband that led to the dissolution of their joint practice, their marriage and the whole life they had shared together. An African-American professional woman with strong spiritual beliefs, Wendy is convinced that God and her deceased father helped her when life seemed at its lowest.

Wendy admits that she was totally shocked when she discovered that her husband was spending their money to appease a severe drug addiction—it was an addiction she had not known about at the time but could certainly see signs of in retrospect. To her sorrow, Wendy discovered that there was nothing she could do to "save" her husband. Rather than choosing to get help for his condition, her husband chose the drugs instead, eventually resulting in their divorce. It wasn't long before she found herself "jobless and penniless." To make matters worse, the social group they had associated with abandoned them both. Because her mother lived in another city and her father had been dead for more than a decade, Wendy felt truly alone. For a time, she couldn't help but feel punished by God.

During her most challenging time, two different sources referred her to a metaphysical group and suggested she might find comfort with them. Although the first time she thought the idea somewhat foreign to her background and upbringing, the second time she heard the suggestion, she decided it was not a coincidence: "I have always said that God has to tell me something twice for me to really hear and understand." The group turned out to be a blessing and helped to replace the social structure she had lost with her husband. However, she still needed to find work.

During her time of greatest depression and crisis, two different sources suggested that she see a local intuitive who specialized in issues related to career and relationships. The first time she heard the suggestion, she simply brushed the idea aside. On another occasion, after she had been crying and felt desperate, she yelled out, "Daddy, please help me . . . I don't know what to do." Although her father had been dead for years, she felt that her father was present and was suggesting that she call one of her dearest friends. Wendy made the call, started to explain her feelings, and the friend's suggestion was to call a local psychic—the same name Wendy had heard previously: "I felt like God was telling me twice."

Wendy followed through and found her session with the psychic to be "a great healing experience." It enabled her to gain a fresh perspective on her life, her failed marriage, and her career. She was encouraged to stand up for herself, to utilize her talents and to begin a new life: "Rather than seeing the experience as a punishment, I truly began to understand that I could see it instead as a valuable lesson. With a new understanding and frame of mind, I was able to work through all of the rough times."

Wendy followed the advice. Rather than remaining victimized by what had happened to her, she decided to start her own practice. The decision proved to be a fruitful one, and her practice has grown tremendously over the years. She has also found a new relationship. She acknowledges that the whole experience proved to be a blessing in disguise:

Life really did begin for me after forty—my whole life perspective and purpose has changed. I am not resentful or remorseful because of the past. I know that this was a spiritual rebirth and awakening for me. My practice has become one in which I feel as if I am being of service—I am able to work with healing, often with Divine guidance. This whole experience enabled me to understand why I was here and what it is I am supposed to be doing . . . When a door closes, a bigger and better one can open—I just needed to have the sense to go through it.

■

Another example is the life story of Darlene Merrill, whose greatest desire was simply to have children. All her life she had yearned to be a mother. Even when she was a child and had the opportunity to play with her friends, she often chose instead to care for her younger siblings because of her love of children. Her friends used to tease her about wanting to stay inside "with the babies" rather than being outside playing with them. Darlene thought that babies were enchanting: "I loved their smell, their innocence and their vulnerability. I always wanted to have children of my own." At sixteen years of age, she became a high school dropout and got married in order to take the next step with her life. Darlene realizes now that she married the wrong man for the wrong reason—she got married in order to become a mother. However, conceiving a child would prove much more difficult than Darlene had ever imagined.

She and her husband tried repeatedly to conceive without success. When a year had passed without any luck, Darlene began seeing doctors who might help her dream become a reality. She followed everything they suggested in order to become pregnant. Finally, after two years of trying, she discovered that she was expecting. The next few months seemed to be everything she had imagined it would be: "I felt so beautiful when I was pregnant. I wanted the whole world to see me carrying a child." Unfortunately, she would not carry the baby to term:

August 24, 1957, my son died just minutes before his birth. I had carried him for five-and-a-half months. I was eighteen years of age. Although the contraction pains were real enough, as was the delivery, the entire experience was like a dream. The medical staff, my friends and my family all tried to make me feel better after the loss, but I really couldn't understand why all the fuss, as I seemed prepared for the baby's death. Even when I went into labor, I accepted it as though it had been ordained. Within a few weeks, life returned to "normal."

Darlene had no better luck with her second pregnancy. Premature contractions, a thinning of the cervix and recurring bleeding were constant issues, as they had been during her first pregnancy. This time, however, she was determined to carry the baby to full term. She persevered, took expensive medication in order to help keep her cervix strong, performed uterus exercises that had been recommended by the doctor and spent considerable time resting in bed. Unfortunately, at six-and-a-half months her contractions began and she was taken to the hospital for a second premature delivery:

When the contractions began this time, I felt much more anguish than I had previously. After all, I had been trying for almost five years to have a baby, and here I was getting ready to lose another one. Although I had carried this baby a month longer than the first one, I wasn't expecting the baby to live. After a difficult delivery, my son was born alive and immediately placed in an incubator. For the next fourteen hours, I was more miserable than I can ever remember. I seemed to be unable to rest or remain in one position. A foreboding feeling about what would happen to my child persisted. Nurses were constantly trying to get me to sleep. They told me that the baby was fine and that I needed to get some rest. They gave me sleeping pills and shots but to no avail. I was so anxious about what was to come that I could not rest. Suddenly, at 2:00 a.m., I experienced a feeling that was not of this world . . .

It was indescribable—the most wonderful, beautiful, glorious, warm, glow of peace that I had ever experienced before or have experienced since that time. At the same time, I understood that my baby would not live. Even though I knew the baby was dying, I felt such a peaceful presence that I was comforted. All of my anxiety and nervousness seemed to disappear. This peaceful presence only lasted a short while, but as soon as it passed, I fell immediately to sleep.

When she awoke the next morning, Darlene found the hospital in the midst of its busy routine: nurses were coming and going, meal trays were being wheeled down the corridors, and so forth. That morning, she could still feel the remnants of the peaceful glow from the night before. At the same time, however, she realized that her wonderful experience at 2:00 a.m. had occurred at the very moment of her son's death. For that reason, it didn't make any sense to her when her obstetrician arrived at 8:30 a.m. and asked if she wanted to go to the nursery to see her baby. She was speechless.

Before she could respond, the doctor excused himself and said that he would return shortly to take her to the nursery. Although still convinced that her son was dead, Darlene began to wonder whether she should question her sanity. A few minutes later, however, another doctor, the pediatrician, came to her room and said that he had something to tell her.

Immediately, Darlene said to him, "My baby is dead, isn't he? He died at 2:00 a.m. this morning."

The doctor looked perplexed but replied, "Yes." He went on to explain that there were twins born at about the same time as her child and that the obstetrician had gotten the babies mixed up in his head when he had visited the nursery earlier. The pediatrician told her that her obstetrician was too upset to come back into the room to tell her himself.

Looking back on the experience, Darlene believes that on the day she was finally able to leave the hospital, she was experiencing what psychologists call "situational schizophrenia":

I thought everyone should somehow be aware of my experience—both the death of my son and the awareness of the peaceful presence. I looked at people on the street, those waiting for buses, and those driving in the cars next to me, all the while thinking that the world must have changed and that everyone should know that my son had died and that things were different. Of course, life was going on as before—unchanged for them but forever changed for me. I had had an experience that no one that I talked to really believed. Perhaps they thought it was simply the result of a grieving mother, but I knew that I had had a personal encounter with the Divine.

Time passed, and in spite of Darlene's realization that her marriage was less than ideal, her determination to have children persisted. There was nothing else that she thought she could do or that she wanted to do. Eventually, the couple decided to pursue adoption. A few years after the second pregnancy, her dreams of motherhood finally came true. She and her husband adopted two children and eventually had another that she carried to full term. Although she finally had the children she had always longed for, her marriage became even more difficult to deal with:

Even during my first two pregnancies, I knew that my marriage was not good. However, I have never been a quitter, and so I was determined to make it work. But I eventually learned that it takes both partners to make a good marriage—one person cannot do it alone. I believed that children could help make the marriage last; little did I know that our marriage was doomed from the beginning and that children would only widen the gap between us. We had nothing in common.

I think our initial attraction was built on lust, not on love. Sometimes it's easy to mistake one for the other. Even after I started thinking that the marriage had been a terrible mistake, I believed it was my responsibility to make the marriage work. I started to become what I thought was the perfect wife. I tried so hard to have that ideal American life—the little white house with the white picket fence. I became the perfect lover, housekeeper, yard-keeper, working woman, etc. and etc. The more I tried to be perfect, however, the more critical my husband became. He began to drink, and I began to believe that he was seeing other women. My insecurities led me to accuse him of everything: lying, cheating, whatever came to mind. He became abusive—emotionally, mentally and physically. He called me dumb and stupid and often laughed at me and slapped me whenever he felt like it.

By the time I was twenty-seven, I had to acknowledge that the marriage was a failure. Nothing seemed to be working. I think that both of us were searching for something that neither of us was able to give to the other. In spite of my experience with the Divine presence in the hospital, I found that I had even given up on God.

The final straw came one night when my husband was, as usual, late for dinner. He called to tell me that he was at a bar with his boss and their secretaries. I told him that I would get a sitter and come to join them. I'll NEVER forget the feeling that came over me when he responded, *"You're not wanted."* I knew then that the marriage was over. I didn't know what I was going to do, but I knew that I had to do something.

The next morning, Darlene took her two youngest children with her and arranged for the neighbor to take care of her eldest son, who was in the first grade. She left South Carolina and headed for Virginia to visit her cousin, Anne, with whom she had grown up and always felt comfortable, "sharing my deepest, darkest concerns and secrets." While at Anne's, she divulged her problems and her feelings. She felt trapped, betrayed, desperate, unloved and alone. She felt that there was nothing she could do to change her life—she had no skills, no future and no money. In spite of her responsibilities as a mother, part of her simply wanted to give up and die. She had little energy and spent the next two weeks slipping in and out of depression while Anne took care of her children: "I just wanted to go to sleep and never ever wake up again."

Anne tried to tell her how much the kids needed her and how much she needed to get back her strength, but Darlene could not be reached. One day Anne insisted that they all go to the beach, and Darlene relented. That day at the beach Darlene would have a second encounter with the Divine:

Anne was sitting on the sand with my kids, and I was walking by myself along the shoreline. I remember feeling small and insignificant. After I had walked a little ways, I looked out at the horizon and spoke to God.

I remember asking for help. I remember asking how I would be able to take care of my children. I had no education and no way to support us. I wanted to get out of the mess that my life had become, but I didn't know how. I remember asking for guidance. I wanted to know what I was supposed to do. Suddenly, something began to happen.

Even though I had not been aware of the sun, all at once it felt very warm and bright. It seemed like answers to the questions I had asked were beginning to flood into my mind. Somehow I could see, hear, even sense the answers to the things that I had been worried about. In spite of my depression and lack of energy, with the answers came more energy than I had possessed in a very long time. In fact, the energy was unlike anything I had ever experienced. Something filled my entire being. The feeling of depression and nothingness disappeared. All at once I felt like I was part of everything: the brilliant, warm rays of the sun, the glistening sand, the beautiful blue sky with the soft, floating clouds and the magnificent, majestic ocean. It seemed like I was at peace and at one with nature. I also had a sense of what I was supposed to do. When I left that beach, I left behind my old self so that when I returned to South Carolina, I felt like a completely different person.

When Darlene returned home, she decided to complete her missing two years of high school at night. She fell in love with learning and soon decided that a high school education would not be enough to properly care for her three children. After receiving her diploma, she enrolled in college and completed a four-year psychology degree program in three years. Six months after graduating from college and finding a job, Darlene was able to divorce her first husband.

Darlene's love for learning persisted. She went on to earn both master's and doctoral degrees in psychology. She also pursued post-graduate work. Rather than being uneducated and unemployed, her life and her choice of careers took a dramatic turn. Over the years, Darlene has had a long and prosperous career with social services, the government and even the penitentiary system, assisting inmates through her work. In fact, in spite of "starting out as a high school dropout," Darlene's career has included roles as a personnel management specialist for the U.S. military, a senior staff advisor for the U.S. Department of Transportation, a counselor and social worker and an advocate for the judicial system, as well as a much sought-after trainer and educator.

In terms of her personal life, after her divorce, she remarried a wonderful, supportive husband. Today, she is the proud mother of three children and three grandchildren. She has been with her second husband for twenty-six years. Darlene says, "Our marriage is wonderful and stronger now than ever; it grows stronger each day that we are together."

In reflecting back upon her life, her personal transformation and her Divine experiences, Darlene offers the following advice:

How did I do it, you ask? I did it by living, by taking risks and by making mistakes—lots of them! I did it by working with forgiveness, including learning how to forgive myself. I did it by studying, by praying, by trying to meditate, by making myself get up every time I thought I was down. I did it by repeatedly trying to do those things that I once believed I could not do.

I've learned so many things since that time. I've learned that my will is not God's will, and I've learned how much more comfortable, wonderful and beautiful life can become when your will and His will for you are aligned. I've learned that although each of us must solve our own problems, we will be given the strength and the guidance to do so, if we simply ask. I've learned the HARD way that the world does not revolve around me but me with it.

I have also learned that everyone is just as important as any other person: the janitor, the priest, the pauper, the millionaire, the ignorant, the educated, the insane, the sane, the prisoner, the "free" man. We are all the same in the sight of God. We are all on the same path, finding our way back to our relationship with Him.

In Darlene's experience and the experience of each of the other individuals who found the Presence of the Divine in the midst of personal hardship, it appears as if God can often be found when there is nowhere else to turn. In the face of some of life's most difficult challenges, when an individual is beaten down by depression, loneliness or hopelessness and finds himself or herself on the verge of giving up, sometimes all that remains is the all-pervading presence of God. And when that Presence becomes felt, it is as if the cares of the world suddenly dissipate and the individual is left with an abundance of peace, comfort and love.

5

Visionary Experiences

Oh Arjuna, whatever is the seed of all beings, that also am I.

Without Me there is no being existent, whether moving or unmoving.

O Parantapa, there is no end to the manifestations of My Divine Power; what I have declared is only a partial statement of the vastness of my Divine manifestation.

Whatever being there is, glorious, prosperous or powerful, know thou that to have sprung from a portion of My splendor . . . I alone exist, sustaining this whole universe by a portion of Myself.

Srimad-Bhagavad-Gita
Divine Manifestation, 85-86

Narendra Nath Datta, often called *Naren* for short, was born on January 12, 1863, in Calcutta to a middle-class family of some prominence and social status. His father was an attorney with the high court in Calcutta, and his mother was a deeply religious woman who raised her children in the spiritual tradition of India. Because the British were in charge of his country at the time, Naren underwent a mostly Western education.

Although schooled in Western thinking and teachings, even as a young man he felt driven to find the true meaning of life. That drive became his foremost desire and led him to study various philosophies and religions. His spiritual quest would eventually enable him to become equally comfortable discussing the Hindu, Buddhist, Jewish, Christian and Islamic scriptures.

As a result of his spiritual search, he met numerous spiritual leaders and holy men. He also began to practice the discipline of meditation. Upon being introduced to various religious leaders, he reportedly asked whether or not they had seen God. Repeatedly, he was met with disappointment until the day came when—at the age of eighteen—he was able to ask the same question of Ramakrishna. Reportedly, when the question was asked, "Sir, have you seen God?" Ramakrishna replied without hesitation, "Yes, I have seen God. I see him as I see you here, only more clearly." (Chetanananda, 11) The response impressed Naren, and although skeptical, he became a close observer and eventual friend and disciple of Ramakrishna's.

Early on in their relationship when Naren wanted Ramakrishna to describe how it was possible for God to be in all things, as was described in the Vedanta scriptures (the philosophy and religion of the Upanishads), Ramakrishna simply reached out and touched him:

> At the marvelous touch of my Master, my mind underwent a complete revolution. I was aghast to realize that there really was nothing whatever in the entire universe but God. I remained silent, wondering how long this state of mind would continue. It didn't pass off all day. I got back home and I felt just the same there; everything I saw was God. I sat down to eat, and I saw that everything—the plate, the food, my mother who was serving it, and I myself—everything was God and nothing else but God . . . It was a kind of intoxication; I can't describe it.
>
> Chetanananda, 19

For five years Naren became educated in spiritual disciplines and the teachings of Ramakrishna. In time, he desired to preach the philosophy of Hinduism to everyone. Naren was especially concerned for the uneducated masses that were shut off from the helpful insights of the Vedanta scriptures because of their inability to read. He was a champion of equality and a respecter of the equal rights of both men and women.

A lifelong student of various religious truths, Naren decided to deeply investigate the teachings of Buddha, for whom he had a special affection. His search eventually led him to visit the Bodhi-tree of Boh-Gaya where the Buddha had reportedly attained enlightenment in the sixth century B.C. After meditating for long hours, Naren became overwhelmed with emotion and started to cry uncontrollably. Explaining what had occurred, he said that while meditating he had become aware of the presence of the Buddha. He also became aware of how immeasurably the history of India had been changed by the Buddha's teachings—such insight and awareness had led to his being unable to control his emotions. (Nikhilananda, 63)

Years later, he would describe an earlier experience in which he believed he had also been in the Buddha's presence:

> While at school, one night I was meditating within closed doors and had a fairly deep concentration of mind . . . When I kept my mind still and devoid of all objects, there flowed in it a current of serene bliss. Under its influence, I felt a sort of intoxication for a long time even after the end of the meditation; so I did not feel inclined to leave my seat and get up immediately. When I was sitting in that condition at the end of the meditation, I saw the wondrous figure of a monk appear suddenly—from where I do not know—and stand before me at a little distance, filling the room with a divine effulgence. He was in ochre robes with a kamandalu [waterpot] in his hand . . . I was amazed and I felt much drawn to him. He walked towards me with a slow step, his eyes steadfastly fixed on me, as if he wanted to say something. But I was seized with fear and could not keep still. I got up from my seat, opened the door, and quickly left the room. The next moment I thought, "Why this foolish fear?" I became bold and went back into the room to listen to the monk, who, alas, was no longer there . . . very often I think that I had the good fortune of seeing Lord Buddha that day.
> Chetanananda, 7

A brilliant student, speaker and leader in his own right, prior to Ramakrishna's death in 1886, Naren was appointed to lead the small Hindu sect. Since it was customary for monks to renounce their names, as well as all other attachments, in time Naren would take the name

Vivekananda. After his Master's death, Ramakrishna appeared to Vivekananda as a brilliant luminous body that remained unseen to the rest of the sect's disciples. Years later, Vivekananda would see Ramakrishna once again during a series of visions that reportedly lasted twenty-one nights in succession.

Bothered by the suffering he saw throughout India, Vivekananda was determined to bring about dramatic spiritual, cultural and economic changes. He began frequent lecture tours throughout his country, speaking for spiritual revival, a regeneration of India's heritage, and the importance of education and hygiene. It was while traveling in India that he heard about the World Parliament of Religions that was being held in Chicago in 1893, bringing together various spiritual and religious leaders from throughout the known world.

When it was suggested that Vivekananda go to Chicago, he flatly refused, but he eventually began to wonder whether or not his path would lead him to the United States. He wrestled with the question repeatedly and worried about the wisdom of leaving behind the work he was trying to do in India. Finally, he asked for a vision as to whether or not he should make the trip. One night, as he was half asleep still pondering the question, he saw a vision of Ramakrishna walking from the seashore of India into the ocean and beckoning for Vivekananda to follow. He needed no further encouragement.

When he arrived in the United States, the deadline for applications to speak at the conference had already passed. In addition, his credentials as a religious leader were not accepted. However, through a series of chance meetings and encounters with important public figures, the deadlines were ignored, his credentials were approved and he was accepted as a representative of Hinduism at the World Parliament of Religions.

He quickly won over his American audiences through his speaking ability, his handsome appearance and his commanding presence. He also praised much that America had accomplished through hard work, cooperation with one another and the application of scientific knowledge. He championed an end to religious bigotry, sectarianism and fanaticism. He believed that all religions could effectively lead their adherents to the same goal of perfection. He believed that ultimately all paths could lead to God. Vivekananda told his audiences, however, that they needed to redefine their concept of religion: " . . . religion does not consist in talk, or doctrines or books, but in realization. It is not learning but *being*." (Chetanananda, 65)

At the heart of his presentations was the belief that the West and the East needed to learn from one another. From the East, the West might learn about spirituality and devotion; from the West, the East might learn about science and cultivating a national spirit. He was against India's caste system, its neglect of the poor and its treatment of women. He was against the West's focus on materialism and money. Vivekananda believed that the two cultures needed to draw what was best from one another.

He addressed the World Parliament approximately a dozen times—speaking to as many as seven thousand individuals at one time. His lectures detailed the ultimate harmony of all religions, the oneness of God, and the divinity of the human soul. During his final presentation, Vivekananda told his audience:

> The Christian is not to become a Hindu or a Buddhist, nor is a Hindu or a Buddhist to become a Christian. But each must assimilate the spirit of the others and yet preserve his individuality and grow according to his own law of growth. If the Parliament of Religions has shown anything to the world, it is this: It has proved to the world that holiness, purity and charity are not the exclusive possession of any church in the world and that every system has produced men and women of the most exalted character. In the face of this evidence, if anybody dreams of the exclusive survival of his own religion and the destruction of the others, I pity him from the bottom of my heart and point out to him that upon the banner of every religion will soon be written, in spite of resistance: "Help, and not Fight," "Assimilation and not Destruction," "Harmony and Peace and not Dissension."
>
> Nikhilananda, 121

After hearing his lectures, the *New York Herald* wrote, "He is undoubtedly the greatest figure in the Parliament of Religions. After hearing him, we feel how foolish it is to send missionaries to this learned nation." Countless other papers reported similar assessments. In a very short time, the unknown monk from Calcutta would become an instant celebrity—life-sized portraits of him were posted throughout the streets of Chicago.

His magnetism and his philosophy caused him to become a sensation. For the next four years he lectured throughout the United States and established the Vedanta Society in New York City as a means of disseminating the universal truths of Hinduism to America. After traveling briefly to England, he returned to India and officially established the Ramakrishna Mission. His work continued in India. He would return to the United States in 1899, as well as take time to travel to Europe and England. In 1900, he returned to his beloved India, where he died two years later on July 4, 1902. To his disciples and adherents, his life would serve as a testimony to the reality of seeing God—a reality that resided within every individual:

> From the earliest times I can remember, I used to see a marvelous point of light between my eyebrows as soon as I shut my eyes to go to sleep, and I used to watch its various changes with great attention. In order to watch it better, I'd kneel on the bed in the attitude a devotee takes when he prostrates before a shine, his forehead touching the ground. That marvelous point of light would change colors and get bigger and bigger until it took the form of a ball; finally it would burst and cover my body from head to foot with white liquid light. As soon as that happened, I would lose outer consciousness and fall asleep. I used to believe that this was the way everybody went to sleep. Then, when I grew older and began to practice meditation, that point of light would appear to me as soon as I closed my eyes, and I'd concentrate upon it. At that time, I was practicing meditation with a few friends . . . We told each other about the visions and experiences we had had. And that was how I found out that none of them had ever seen that point of light or gone to sleep in that way.
>
> Chetanananda, 6

Although he lived to be only thirty-nine years old, Vivekananda would become the foremost disciple of the Hindu spiritual leader, Ramakrishna, the individual most responsible for bringing much of Eastern philosophy to the Western world, and perhaps the most influential figure in the nineteenth century revival of Hinduism.

■

A visionary experience of his own led Tom Andrews to believe that there was much more to the concepts of space and time then he had ever imagined. In fact, the encounter helped to completely change his concept of God:

I had always questioned the God I was taught about as a child—a vengeful out-to-get-you God. However, after my experience, I came to realize and *know* God as omnipresent, all powerful and all loving—a Creator concerned with each and every soul that is a spark of the Divine.

Raised in a fairly conservative household, Tom remembers a recurring experience as a child that seemed as natural to him "as riding a bicycle." At night when he was supposed to be falling asleep, he found that he could leave his body and float around the room—looking down at his own body. Rather than understanding the uniqueness of these childhood experiences, Tom says, "I never gave it a second thought—I didn't think of it as being odd or unusual. It was just something I could do." Eventually, the ability left him, but it may have been part of the impetus that caused him to begin a lifelong search for truth—a search that has led him to many spiritual paths and truths that he now embraces as his own.

Tom's visionary encounter occurred when he was in his twenties during a day when he was by himself at home in the Oklahoma countryside. He had been taking a nap on the couch when he heard a loud "THUMP, THUMP" that startled him awake:

I live alone in the country, so I was quickly brought to my senses. It sounded like someone was stomping very hard on one of my wood floors. All at once I heard it again, "THUMP, THUMP." I was fully awake and scared, and when I turned, I could see a beautiful, radiant woman sitting on the couch across from me. She appeared as a Native American woman with long, black hair hanging loose over her shoulders. She had a red blanket wrapped around her, and she was calmly petting a large, white wolf, which was sitting on the floor. She looked at me intensely, and I felt a warm feeling of love. Intuitively, I somehow knew that she was checking on me to see how I was progressing on my spiritual journey. After that, she disappeared and I was left alone.

The amazing experience prompted Tom to look into his ancestral background. As a result, he discovered that he is a descendant of Cherokee people from the Wolf Clan. Since that time, Tom believes that the Native American woman he saw was a vision of a spirit guide.

Over the years his interest in Native American spirituality has grown, and he has been responsible for holding monthly sweat lodge ceremonies on his property:

I live in the southeastern part of the state with lots of trees and rolling hills. The Creator put me in touch with a full-blooded Choctaw spiritual leader who had been seeking a place to build a sweat lodge.

We have been having a sweat at least once a month. Here, through the rain, sleet and snow, we have a host of people who come and pray with us. The Creator has healed many, and we have had many blessings poured out onto us.

When asked to describe the connection he feels toward the small group of people that meet regularly on his property, Tom says simply, "This little group of people have enriched my life. We have found what millions are looking for."

■

Bernice Rawlins had her own visionary experience that came as a result of her work with healing prayer. A longtime student of spirituality and healing, Bernice has studied a variety of disciplines, including meditation, Therapeutic Touch, healing touch, prayer healing, and bodywork.

The experience occurred when Bernice was having a great deal of difficulty in her marriage. In spite of the challenges she was having with a husband, whom she would later divorce, she continued working with her commitment to healing prayer. It was a commitment she often discussed with her closest friends.

One evening Bernice received a phone call from a friend who was very upset. The friend said that a woman named Donna had just been in a very serious automobile accident. Doctors did not know whether Donna was going to live. The friend asked Bernice to pray.

As soon as she had hung up the phone, Bernice closed her eyes, asked for the Divine presence and began to pray. She followed her normal prayer routine, but this time something different started to occur. After praying for a few moments, Bernice began to visualize Donna lying on a table surrounded by angels. Although the image surprised her, Bernice continued to pray. Even in the midst of her prayers, what Bernice saw next caused her to well up inside with emotion:

All at once I saw Mother Mary. She was wearing sapphire blue clothing and appeared as an incredibly radiant vision. I could not see her face, but I knew with every fiber of my being that it was she. Words cannot really explain how deeply I was affected by her presence, but by this time tears were streaming down my face.

Mother Mary approached the table, and Bernice saw the energy of light, love and radiant healing enter into the injured woman's body. All at once, Mary asked the injured woman a question:

Mary asked Donna whether she wanted to stay and continue her life on earth or whether she wanted to leave her body behind and move on.

Donna said she wanted to stay.

The prayers continued, and I asked that the healing would continue even after I ended the prayer session. The tears were still streaming down my face. When I finally finished, I was left feeling healed, myself, and deeply grateful for the experience.

The next day, Bernice received a call from her friend stating that Donna had stabilized and that doctors seemed more hopeful. Later, a second call revealed how surprised doctors seemed to be with the swiftness of Donna's recovery. It was not long before Donna had fully recuperated from the life-threatening accident. Bernice has no doubt that her experience with Mother Mary and healing was real.

■

Another encounter with Mary occurred in the life of Heather Young, who was not even Catholic: "I was brought up with no particular religious beliefs and was often confused about my own religious feelings at the time." Although she had some close friends who were members of the Catholic Church, Heather admits, "I never really felt completely comfortable with Catholicism."

At the time of her experience, Heather says she was suffering from depression and had hit rock bottom. A year-and-a-half earlier she had been in a terrible car accident with her best and dearest friend. Heather had survived the accident; her best friend had not been so lucky. Because of her despair after the accident, Heather knew she was in trouble: "I knew I needed serious help—I had seen both a social worker and a psychiatrist." She didn't know what she believed, and she didn't know what she wanted to be when she grew up.

One day, her Catholic friends had asked her to accompany them to hear a visionary, who was reportedly able to describe spiritual realities and the certainty of the Divine presence. The experience occurred on October 13—a day that turned out to be the Catholic feast day of the Virgin Mary. The visionary was inspirational; he also discussed the presence of Mary during the program. Heather had taken her camera that day and took several pictures of the group, the outdoors and even the sky. After the event, her troubles seemed much lighter.

Weeks later when she finally had the pictures developed, she became excited at several of the pictures that seemed to possess the shadow of a Divine presence:

I have shown these pictures to everyone I know, and some of my friends are a bit skeptical, but there is no doubt in my mind that somehow the camera caught three pictures of Mary. In the first photo of a statue, there is a shadow of the Virgin Mary as plain as day—there is no mistaking it for something else. In the second, you can clearly make out the same presence. The third picture, although somewhat more faded than the other two, shows the very same thing.

She has no doubt that the experience and the pictures have enabled her to get on with her life. According to Heather, "I was going through a confusing time. I wasn't certain about religion or my future. The experience gave me a whole new perspective about religion."

She became involved in a local Unity Church and began reading a variety of books on "becoming enlightened to the spiritual side of life." She started meditating and praying, and she became convinced of the presence of Guardian Angels. She began to work at healing herself and soon felt well enough to stop her therapy. By her own account, "I have never been happier in my life than I have in the past couple of years." Currently back in school, Heather is on her way to earning a teaching degree because "I have decided that my calling is to be a teacher."

■

In the case of Roger Hahn, a visionary encounter eventually led to an awareness of his ability to work with healing. According to Roger, "The encounter made me more aware that I had a mission in life that would unfold to me at the right time." The experience occurred many years ago, but Roger states, "It's as clear to me as if it had happened yesterday":

I was sitting and meditating. All at once, I became aware of a small, bright light off in the distance that grew bigger and bigger. I found myself floating toward the light to meet it. I found the white light totally loving and exhilarating.

As I moved closer, I could see Jesus standing in the light. It was so peaceful and so beautiful that I just wanted to stay because I felt so good all over.

Christ looked at me as if he wanted me to do something, but he didn't talk. While in this experience, I began to wonder what he wanted me to do, and it was then that the vision started to fade.

Prompted by his experience to discover his life "mission," Roger began a search that eventually led to the awareness of his interest in the healing arts. Today, he is known as a healer and is in the process of establishing his own wellness and healing center. Still inspired by his visionary encounter with the Christ, Roger affirms, "I have found that my soul has a work to do."

■

A social worker named Nora Armstrong had a visionary encounter of her own that enabled her to get over a breakup that had left her completely distraught. She was experiencing a great deal of pain and suffering because her boyfriend had suddenly decided to end their four-year relationship. As a result, Nora says she was devastated and began asking the fundamental question of life: "Why was I here?" The search to answer that question led her to a set of books called *A Course in Miracles.*

Nora began reading "The Course" and found comfort as well as a whole new way of perceiving and thinking about life. Although she had been somewhat successful working through her grief, one day while jogging she found that her fears, her depression and her sense of loss had suddenly returned:

I was jogging on a track that I often went to at the local high school. As I was jogging, some of the questions that had been on my mind for months after breakup returned—questions like "Why did my breakup happen? What was the purpose of my being here? Why did I feel so alone?" The feelings of hurt, sadness and anger returned, and I felt totally alone. To my surprise, I suddenly saw people up ahead of me—people who were not really there.

I saw glowing, luminous bodies on the track. They were all in front of me, and there were hundreds of them. As I watched them moving on the track in front of me, I felt a gentle lift take hold of both of my shoulders. I immediately felt a feeling of lightness and a profound sense of connection and love. It was an incredible experience.

I have to admit that I was mystified by what happened and I thought about it for several weeks thereafter.

A few weeks later, Nora became excited when she came across a passage in *A Course in Miracles* that seemed to perfectly describe her experience:

> As we go along, you may have many "light episodes." They may take many different forms, some of them quite unexpected. Do not be afraid of them. They are signs that you are opening your eyes at last. They will not persist, because they merely symbolize true perception . . .
> *Course,* "Workbook," 25

Nora became convinced that the experience was a Divine encounter and that she was well on her way to healing. The experience proved invaluable at helping her work through the remnants of her grief. She also learned to live in the present and to turn loose of her regrets about the past. When asked to describe why the experience may have happened to her, Nora adds:

> I know that it happened to me to provide reassurance that I was not alone. It also enabled me to understand that there was far more to the world than I had ever realized and that it was possible to be supported by something beyond one's self. The message I felt was that we are all loved unconditionally by God and supported and guided at every moment, if we only choose to perceive it. We all have an inner guidance that we can tap into for any kind of concern, question or issue we may be facing . . .
>
> I believe that we are connected on a soul level. We all have a unique Divine purpose for being here—our journey is simply to discover it and to follow that purpose. Even when we discover blocks to fulfilling that purpose or obstacles in our path, we can always choose again.

■

It was during the most challenging period in her life that Darlene Hill had a visionary experience of her own. At the time, she was having many health problems and was under constant stress because she was trying to deal with and help her rebellious son. Darlene explains it simply as "I was going through a very troubling time."

Because of her health problems, her many medications were taking their toll on her physical body. Her son was also pushing her to the edge of her sanity. The side effects of her health, the stress and the medications were testing her to the limit, and Darlene felt that she was on the verge of a nervous breakdown. Feeling physically sick, very much alone and at her wit's end, Darlene remembers that a day came when she gathered her pills together and went outside:

I couldn't cope any more. I was up against a brick wall. Not knowing where else to turn, I decided to talk to God as a last resort. I carried my pills and all of my troubles and went out to the middle of the field on my property. I started to talk to God and literally begged Him to help me because I couldn't go on.

While I was pouring my heart out to God, I began to notice this golden glitter falling out of the sky. It wasn't my imagination. It started falling all over me. It was absolutely beautiful!

I touched it, caught it like snowflakes and rubbed it into my skin. It made me happy just to feel it against me. I stayed there for quite some time. The whole while, the gold glitter continued to fall.

Suddenly I realized that I didn't feel sick—I felt physically good for the first time in a long while! I also realized that I was no longer troubled by my problems with my son. A great weight had suddenly been lifted off of me. Before I returned to the house, I threw the pills away. I would never need them again. I was well.

Darlene calls the experience "the beginning of a life change for me." After she pondered what had happened to her for a few weeks, she decided that she needed to "find out more about God." That search led her to the books *The Art of Meditation* and *The Infinite Way*, by Joel Goldsmith. As a result of reading the books, Darlene began to teach herself and practice meditation. Although she had a hard time with the discipline, Darlene persisted. She made herself do it every day at the same time. She recalls what happened next:

One day I was practicing my meditation like I usually did, when something started to happen. I felt my whole body start to tingle. At first I thought I might be having a heart attack. The experience felt good, but it was strange, so I stopped meditating that day. However, when I was meditating the next day, the same thing started to happen. Instead of stopping the meditation, this time I kept going. What an experience I had!

I suddenly felt like I was totally surrounded by golden, swirling clouds. As I watched, the clouds formed a tunnel—I was drawn along by the swirling. I started seeing things passing by me very quickly. I could see other beings—some had bright auras around them; others were all light. I had no idea where I was, but every day in meditation I would go to this place.

During her waking moments, Darlene began practicing a discipline that had been recommended by Joel Goldsmith—trying to keep her mind on God all of the time:

I started doing just that. It is the hardest thing in the world to do, but in every waking moment I did just that. If any thoughts other than God came into my mind, I hummed a special song to keep those thoughts out. When I awoke in the morning, the first thing I thought about was God, and I thanked Him. The last thing I did at night was think of Him and thank Him.

Everything that I did, I did to praise God. Everything that I did was done to the best of my abilities, with God always in mind. After a couple of weeks of this, I started having the most beautiful dreams.

There were always people around me in the dreams, pouring love out to me. I awoke each morning filled with love. During the day, I was given so much guidance it seemed that if I had any question, it was answered immediately.

One of Darlene's final visions came when she was doing her "meditation walk" after dinner around her property:

I started my walk just as I usually did. I walked along thanking God for the beautiful day and praising Him. As I walked, I noticed all of the beautiful flowers in my path. They were everywhere. When I looked up at the sky, I saw two angels facing each other . . . what a beautiful sight. Suddenly they faded, and a giant, golden Buddha covered the sky . . .

Later, I felt a feeling of intense love coming over me. It was a feeling that words can't describe. I simply accepted this beautiful gift that God was giving to me.

Darlene admits that she has never again recaptured the sense of love that filled her being during the period when she had been able to keep her mind on God all of the time, but she admits that she really hasn't tried:

Someone asked me once why I didn't try to get those feelings back. I told them that you can't really live with those feelings all of the time here on the earth plane. I would be running up and down the streets hugging and kissing everyone that I met. It is a love you have for everyone and everything, and it is indescribable.

God gave me a very beautiful gift during that time. I was healed, and I had the opportunity to commune with Him. I feel very luck and happy. And I know one day I will recapture those same feelings of love . . . when I go home to be with Him.

■

In another case, a woman named Thelma Jacobs is quick to point out that her upbringing in a conservative church did not really prepare her for her visionary encounter that occurred later in life. Although she and her husband met at a Baptist Sunday school, within ten years of their marriage they had begun to explore various spiritual traditions, metaphysics and the practice of meditation. Eventually, they came across the Edgar Cayce material and became very much involved in the Cayce work—taking part in conferences and spiritual growth discussion groups. According to Thelma, "all of these events changed our lives!"

Always interested in art, after her roles as a wife and mother, Thelma pursued art education and her own career as a painter. It is an occupation that fulfills her on many levels—an all-encompassing process that often touches her body, mind and soul. On one occasion, Thelma remembers having finished a painting when a Divine presence unexpectedly appeared in her studio:

> I had just completed an impressionistic painting, and my husband and I were sitting in my studio. The painting was still on the easel. Suddenly, I saw a smiling angel standing close to my painting. She was extremely beautiful and was smiling at me.

Thelma was dumbfounded and could not believe what she was seeing. She simply stared back at the angel and remained silent: "I can still see her in my mind's eye. She had the most beautiful face and smile. I saw her only for a few moments, but I have no doubt that I saw what I saw."

As if to confirm her experience, a few months later Thelma was attending a conference program that featured a talented psychic. Without telling the woman of her encounter, the psychic told Thelma, "Angels often surround you when you paint."

Since that time, Thelma says, "Because of what I saw and because the psychic told me about the presence of angels, I now meditate and pray before I begin painting." She adds, "My experience with the angel is something I will *never* forget!"

■

Wanda Grange is convinced that she had her own encounter with Jesus during the first year of her marriage to a very difficult and challenging husband. The newlywed couple was poor and from very different backgrounds—each element adding its own stress to their relationship.

Wanda's husband was an immigrant from Togo, West Africa. He was also extremely forceful in manner and very self-assured. Wanda, on the other hand, had low self-esteem, was meek by comparison and often found herself cowering next to her husband's powerful personality.

The first few months of their marriage were filled with numerous arguments—often causing her husband to become enraged, critical and verbally abusive. During those experiences, Wanda often found herself questioning her worth as a wife rather than wondering about the appropriateness of her husband's temper.

An enormous argument occurred one day when her husband had been asked to give a public lecture on his native country. Wanda had planned to go to the lecture to support her husband, but in the midst of the argument her husband forbade her to go, stating that she had made him angry and that he wanted to go by himself. When he left their apartment without her, Wanda was devastated. She recalls:

I felt like a total jerk and a failure as a wife. I was facedown on our dirty, old rug in our roach-infested apartment. I was crying and praying for Jesus to come and help me because I felt like I had been a good, devoted follower since I had been a young child.

Although Wanda had been sobbing profusely, all at once something within her changed instantly:

I suddenly felt uplifted, somehow. I opened my eyes and could see the eyes of Jesus in front of me. I could see only his eyes, but they were loving and beautiful.

Next I saw a scene that was like a Peter Max painting—a simplistic scene of green grass, wildflowers and sunshine. I could see thick woods in the distance, and I somehow knew that I was entering a difficult period in my life. However, I didn't care because I was so happy that I could see Jesus' eyes.

Even in the midst of her experience, Wanda found herself reverting to her feelings of worthlessness:

I felt ashamed that I had cried out for Jesus to come, as though I were a spoiled child. I didn't feel worthy to be able to see him. I was happy he had come, but I was still ashamed for not trusting that he would hear my prayers.

The experience encouraged Wanda to pursue an interest in spirituality and to continue to work on herself, even while in the challenging relationship. Regardless of how she felt treated by her husband, Wanda could recall, "Jesus cared enough about me to actually show up."

Although it took time to come to the realization, for her own health Wanda eventually understood that her best course of action in her personal life was a divorce. She followed through on what she knew she had to do and has become a stronger person because of it. Since that time, her sense of self-worth has gradually improved, and Wanda states that she has learned to become more trusting of her own abilities and less fearful of life. She also says, "I have learned that I can expect an answer to my prayers."

■

Brian Keeley experienced a personal vision in his own life that left him "forever changed." Describing himself as "an only child born to a typical middle class couple," most of Brian's church-going experience was Southern Baptist. A computer programmer for a major bank, Brian believes that an involuntary out-of-body experience prompted his personal encounter with the Divine.

Although Brian had been simply standing at his kitchen doing dishes, a moment later his perception shifted to a completely different vantage point:

I suddenly saw myself from an elevated, oblique angle—almost as if I were seeing myself through the eyes of a fly perched up in the corner of the room. Gradually, the field of view began to widen and pull back, as if a camera were zooming out. I saw myself in my house; I zoomed out further to see my house on the block; zoomed out further until my house was a dot in the city; zoomed out until the city was a dot on the Eastern seaboard. This zooming effect began to move outward, faster and faster until the earth became a dot and then the sun followed close behind. Stars went by, becoming smaller and smaller until they merged together and began to look like smoky wisps. Finally, this outward zoom stopped, and in front of me was our entire galaxy.

A small, white pulsing dot appeared and highlighted where our sun was located within one of the spiral arms of our Milky Way galaxy. The galaxy before me was then tilted to afford a better view of it from an oblique angle.

During this experience, Brian says he became aware of at least three other forms of civilizations in the universe. He associated these life forms with colors from the spectrum and somehow "knew" truths about each of them. According to Brian, he became aware that the "blue" civilization and the "yellow" civilization were far more advanced than humankind. The "red" civilization seemed to be the oldest but also seemed to be inhabited with a life form that was like "grumpy old people that wanted to be left alone." After perceiving these civilizations, Brian zoomed outward again and was shown "the actual fabric of the universe."

When the outer expansion stopped, the process reversed itself. Brian began to zoom in, closing in on the galaxy, the earth, the city and his home. However, rather than stopping, it continued until he became aware of an atom that compressed even further until he was shown "the most primordial component of matter," which he describes simply as "energy." The experience continued until Brian experienced "the most amazing thing":

> For one brief moment, an exact instant in time, a fraction of a second, smaller than has ever been measured, I was granted complete and God-like understanding of all that I had been shown. I hadn't just seen it; I KNEW it. I understood EVERYTHING. I understood all of the physical laws and forces that comprise the universe. I understood the role everything from the largest to the smallest structure in the universe played in its functioning. An infinite number of interactions and dependencies were as easily understood as the rules to a tick-tack-toe game. It was simple, pure knowing . . . knowing of everything as it existed at that exact moment.
>
> And then I "awoke" to regular consciousness.

Brian found himself standing in his house still working on the same dish he had been washing. The God-like understanding was gone. He remembered the experience, and he remembered that for a fleeting instant he had known everything, but it was gone.

Brian is not certain why he had the visionary experience, calling it simply "some kind of a gift." The result of it, however, has been that he now has no doubt other life exists in the universe. He also knows first-hand that the universe was created by design, not chaos. Since that time, he has gained a reverence for the good in all religious teachings, rather than focusing on their differences. Most of all, he has come to believe that God simply is:

I got no impression of God being only a Jewish God, a Catholic God, a Protestant God, an Islamic God, or any other labels we have placed on our religious systems. God simply is. We put labels or conventions on God in an attempt to provide a more conventional reference that we might more easily understand, but God simply is.

6

Experiencing the Divine in Nature

In the beginning there was Existence, One only, without a second . . . He, the One, thought to himself: Let me be many, let me grow forth.

Thus out of himself he projected the universe;
and having projected out of himself the universe,
he entered into every being. All that is has its self in him alone.

Of all things he is the subtle essence. He is the truth. He is the Self.

The Upanishads
Chandogya, 68–69

Mildred Sechler was born in Allentown, Pennsylvania on May 10, 1909. Even as a child she seemed to possess a keen awareness far beyond the perception of most individuals. This awareness enabled her to see a world just beyond the range of most individuals—she could see energy, forms of light and angels. In time, her clairvoyant abilities and her apparent communication with the angelic realms in nature and in every aspect of Creation would lead her to become known as a twentieth century Christian mystic. For nearly seventy years, until her death in 1994, Mildred would pledge her life to increasing the world's knowledge of angels and the value of non-sectarian New Age truths and Christian mysticism.

By her own account, when she was six years old, Mildred stood against the railing of the Staten Island Ferry on its way to the New York Harbor. Her face became illuminated with enthusiasm and joy as she pointed out over the railing to the top of the water and exclaimed, "Oh, look at the beautiful fairies!" (Isaac, 45) Through her young eyes she could see dozens of tiny fairies, called *water sprites*, dancing atop the water's surface. With a friend at the time, Mildred was stunned when she realized that her friend could not see the dancing fairies. In time, the fact that her visionary experiences seemed to be hers alone led her to the unmistakable conclusion that she "saw a world that other people didn't." (Isaac, 46)

Raised in a Christian environment with a strong Quaker influence, Mildred had long believed in the presence of Guardian Angels. Therefore, it came as no surprise to her when, at the age of ten, her Guardian Angel appeared to her and stated, "It is now my task to take the responsibility of your life's instruction." (Isaac, 50) At the age of thirteen, following the prompting of her Guardian, Mildred explained to her mother and sister (her father had died years before) that she no longer wished to be called *Mildred* but instead *Flower*—the name would stick for the rest of her life.

That same year she would see her first ghost—an eighteenth century sailor who apparently did not know that he was dead. Following her Guardian's instruction, Flower helped the man pass from the lower realms of the "astral world" to the other side. Her clairvoyant abilities continued to grow, enhancing her perception and opening her up to a world that others might only imagine. Rather than being regarded as simply the creative musings of a young child, however, her information proved so helpful and accurate that several schoolteachers asked her to discuss her information, her wisdom and the workings of clairvoyance. Their invitation would lead to a lifetime of teaching and lecturing. Known for her insight, even Flower's mother frequently followed through on the young woman's guidance—even going so far as to move the family from Pennsylvania to California when Flower announced, at fifteen, that it was what the family was supposed to do.

At the age of sixteen, Flower began giving regular lectures in "Truth" from her home, as well as in the local Unity Church. So inspiring were her lectures that she began to speak five times a week, soon earning enough from her spiritual teachings that she was able to support her family. In addition to providing information on spirituality and the angelic realms, Flower's mystical insights expanded, and she was able to recall various memories of past lives in places like Persia, Egypt and Greece.

As she grew, so did her clairvoyant abilities. The world she witnessed became one of boundless light, pulsating with the spark of Creation. She could see the human aura as easily as she could see the energy associated with thought and feeling. In time, the entire angelic hierarchy became as visible to her as the mundane world was to others. The life forms Flower perceived included all imaginable creatures from "elementals" and "nature beings" to "devas" and "archangels." She would come to realize that in addition to Guardian Angels for individuals, there were angelic beings for every plant, every creature, every aspect of nature and even every country. Once, when asked to describe the appearance of an angel, she replied:

> In their appearance, the Celestial Inhabitants are quite different from ourselves. In every respect they are larger than humans. One must adjust to new conceptions of size in order to appreciate the Higher Ones. There are Angels that are thirty feet in height and we have watched great Rulers whose bodies were as huge as the mountains they enshrouded. This is true of the Being who envelopes Mount Rainer. The faces of most of the Angelic Beings are rather elongated. Their eyes can be likened to deep pools and occasionally flashes of lightening. Angels absorb electricity from the etheric regions and this sustains them in the same way oxygen sustains us. An impression one has while observing these beings is to yearn for the tremendous vitality with which they are endowed. The celestial workers are always joyous, confident and sympathetic. This is natural, when we realize their ever-present attunement to the Presence of the Most High from Whom flows all that is good. Newhouse, Insights into Reality, 17

On another occasion, while discussing the angels she could see caring for humanity, Flower had the following to say:

> All Angels are beautiful beyond imagining. Masculine Angels are

> overpowering in their magnificent power, joyousness and love. Feminine Angels change anyone who sees them through their transforming embodiments of truth, devotion, and grace. Guardian Angels are no exception; they are all the beauties of love. Their auras are pink—in varying tones according to the needs of their wards. Their hair and eye colors resemble human colors . . .
>
> Guardians are with their wards during every day of their earth lives. They may grow frustrated over their charges' perversities, but they never tire. Seventy or eighty years are like days to them, for there is no time in the mental plane where their consciousness usually resides . . . One has the same Guardian throughout every incarnation . . .
>
> Watcher Angels, on the other hand, are not with their charges constantly. These Angels are in training to be Guardians, and they have several probationary humans in their care. Watchers closely supervise their charges when meeting a testing of evil forces. They stay to help their wards through these times by prompting, uplifting, inspiring, and teaching. Constantly aware of each charge's thoughts and circumstances, Watcher Angels are able to accompany each person in their care during times of need.
>
> Newhouse, Answers, 131-132

At the age of twenty-one, a vision of the Christ would confirm her soul's mission: she was to become a teacher of Christian mysticism and to help humankind understand its higher reality as well as to "become more aware of the Angel Kingdom." (Isaac, 67) In time, Flower would write numerous books on the angelic realms including *Natives of Eternity*, *Rediscovering the Angels*, and *Kingdom of the Shining Ones*.

In 1933, a young man named Lawrence Newhouse attended one of her lectures. Flower recognized a soul connection with him immediately, as well as several past-life experiences they had shared, and the two were married that same year—Flower Sechler became Flower Newhouse. Extremely supportive of his wife's work, Lawrence was able to work on the road. During the first five years of their marriage, he helped her visit over one hundred cities, enabling her to share her insights and teachings with others.

In 1940, Lawrence and Flower Newhouse managed to buy over 400 acres in Escondido, California for the establishment of a spiritual center to disseminate Flower's lectures, teachings and writings. It became known as the Questhaven Retreat and the home of the Christward Ministry. Its mission was set down by Flower Newhouse on dedication day and continues to this day and includes increasing the recognition of the reality of Spirit in the earth and enabling individuals to awaken to their own Christ Consciousness and personal enlightenment. (Isaac, 89)

Throughout her life, Flower Newhouse believed that all of Creation acted at its best as it served and worshipped God. Not only was this worship of God the ultimate calling for every human being regardless of his or her religious background but it was also a natural calling for every kingdom of Creation, including angels, devas, elementals and fairies:

> Infinitely soul-stirring are unexpected glimpses of Angelic Orders at their work. Almost resolutely, I daily confine myself to labors at my desk, while outside, little builders are gaily gliding in and about our flower garden. Occasionally I steal to the windows of our study for a sight of those fairy beings, and the joy that swells up from within as I watch those tiny servers is both relaxing and refreshing.
>
> At night, when we have taken our dogs and cats for a long walk in the foothills, we have found ourselves suddenly in the presence of glorious company. One evening a walk was lengthened so that I might observe a being of considerable size who proved to be a director of the Weather Angels. The communications between this Superior and His commands were lost to me, but, along with the Nature Devas, my higher sensibilities were quickened by this Great One's appearance.
>
> It has been joyful, too, when near our cottage to see the silent, loving figure of the Angel of the Home. Her duties of renewing the etheric forces are usually performed when we are away from the home either in body or in spirit while asleep. There are many homes that have Angels protecting them. There are numerous individuals who, when they walk into the countryside, are

companioned by pure presences. Our part is to greet them and to love them even though their forms are still invisible to our physical sight.

At Snoqualmie Falls in Washington State we have observed a Water Guardian as tall as the height of the falls. Such beings are usually of tremendous size and are of very advanced unfoldment. The younger elementals, who pass through the aura of such a being, gain a considerable surcharge of renewal.

It is interesting to watch what takes place in the superphysical aspect of the culture of flowers and growing things. While beautiful builders pour their energies into unfolding blossoms, others busy themselves with the tasks of opening leaves and stirring the flow of life energy through the plant and root system.

Imaginative accounts of the service of builders fill the story books of children. Fairy tales are often based upon verities of nature's actual superphysical activities.

Newhouse, Rediscovering, 34–35

For more than twenty years, Lawrence supported his wife and became an important influence in the establishment and permanence of the Questhaven Retreat center. When he died of cancer in 1963, Flower Newhouse continued to feel his presence and to see him on occasion, but her work of lecturing and writing took the greater part of her energies. For the next thirty years she would continue to inspire audiences with her speaking ability and confirm the realities of the angelic life forms through her books and her lectures. When she died in 1994, she left behind a work that continues to draw individuals from around the world interested in spiritual mysticism and the Angelic Kingdoms. Even today, individuals gather for programs and activities inspired by her life and information at the Questhaven Retreat center in Escondido, California. For many individuals, the life of Flower Newhouse confirms the ongoing work of the Divine in all of Nature and in every aspect of Creation.

■

A contemporary account of a mystical encounter in nature is the story of Joshua Vincent, who experienced a Divine presence in a sunrise when he was twenty-two years old. The encounter was surprising because although his family had raised him in the Christian religion, by the time he was a teenager he had become an atheist. In fact, Joshua admits that he "enjoyed nothing quite as much as attacking the religious beliefs of others." In addition to being an atheist, because of the difficulties he had relating to his parents, other members of his family and his peers, he describes himself as also being "very angry, self-willed and bitter."

While in college his anger and disdain for religion led to an argument with his best friend in which he vehemently attacked his friend's religious beliefs. The result was that they became bitter enemies, and, according to Joshua, "My contempt for him was such that I never spoke to him again."

On the day he graduated, Joshua was hitchhiking home from college when a man driving a Cadillac pulled over and offered him a ride. During the drive home, the man said that he had been an all-American football player. In addition, he had experienced quite a measure of financial success. From appearances, the man seemed happy, content, successful and inspiringly optimistic. Intrigued, Joshua wanted to know the source of the man's accomplishments. The driver attributed his success to the fact that he was religious. Rather than responding with his normal antagonism, Joshua simply listened. Before the drive was over, the man had given Joshua a copy of the book, *Release*, by Starr Daily, dealing with a prisoner's Divine encounter that changed his life forever. Joshua said that he would read it.

True to his word, Joshua read the book but admits, "I didn't quite see how it applied to me." He started a job in journalism with the local newspaper and went on with his life. It was a job that demanded he arrive early each morning, often driving to work just as the sun was coming up. One morning, shortly after starting the new job, he would have a mystical encounter of his own:

As I drove to work, I noticed the beauty of the approaching sunrise. It was so beautiful that I decided to pull off to the side of the road and get out of the car to watch. As the sun touched the tip of the horizon, I began to feel strangely ecstatic. At the same time, my mind felt as if it were expanding. As my mind seemed to expand, my sense of ecstasy increased until the ecstasy was beyond belief. I soon entered a state of mind that I can best describe as a vacuum in which neither time nor space seemed to exist. The most important aspect of this state of mind was the new sense of reality that I felt. I felt far more real, somehow. This state of mind was to my ordinary consciousness as my ordinary consciousness was to a dream. I felt as if I had "woken up" in a manner of speaking and that life as I knew it was some sort of illusion.

At the apex of this experience, a voice boomed in my ears, seeming to come neither from outside of me nor within me but rather strangely from somewhere in between. The voice said: "Seek and ye shall find, ask and it shall be given, knock and it shall be opened unto you." Naturally, I recognized these words as the words of Christ. I was astonished. In that moment of time, I changed from a confirmed atheist to the Christian I am today.

The experience put Joshua on a seeker's path that continues to this day—more than forty years later. By his own admission, since that time he has "explored probably every spiritual path known to man." His interests have expanded to include astrology, metaphysics and New Age spiritual discussion groups.

One aftermath of Joshua's experience since that time has been the fact he has been trying to achieve the same sense of spiritual bliss he once felt for those few fleeting moments as he watched the sunrise. As a result, sometimes he feels stuck between the world of the material and the world of the spiritual. Doubtful, perhaps, that he will ever again have another experience, Joshua nevertheless admits, "I am now, and will always remain, a seeker, until the day I die."

■

When her own Divine encounter occurred, Hannah Glidner found herself in the midst of a great deal of stress both at home and at work. Newly separated from her husband, she was very anxious about the fact that her meager secretarial salary was insufficient to help support her and her two small children. Her husband was not present for her or the children, either emotionally or physically. When the possibility for a promotion opened up at her company, Hannah applied.

She was interviewed and hired immediately. Because of the promotion, her salary was increased an amazing sixty percent, enabling her to set aside many of her worries. Hannah felt that she had been given the break she needed to make things work. Her joy was short-lived, however.

Within a few weeks of her promotion, another employee filed a formal grievance against the company, stating that Hannah had been unfairly promoted to the position. Apparently the other employee had enough of a case to cause Hannah to be formally removed from the position and told that she would have to reapply. Because of the formal charges, rather than allowing her boss to make the selection, the position would now be filled by a committee of eight handling the interview and selection process. In addition to the financial hardship, according to Hannah, "the whole experience was a terrible blow."

In spite of her shock and humiliation, Hannah decided to follow through on reapplying for the position. With the help of some friends, she made preparations to go through the committee process. To be sure, the fact that she had been removed from the position made her feel anxious about whether or not she could pass the committee interview, let alone be hired for the position. When the day came for her formal interview, Hannah drove to the company: "As I drove down the road on the way to the interview, I remember praying very hard. It was not my habit to ask God for a sign, but this time I did because I was struggling for an answer as to why this job had been taken away from me." To Hannah's surprise, as she approached her destination, she noticed "an enormous double rainbow hanging over the building." She had no doubt that it was the sign she had asked for. It gave her the encouragement she had sought because the experience convinced her that God was mindful of her needs. With the appearance of the rainbow, Hannah says she was able to go into the interview feeling very calm and peaceful.

The interview took place, and Hannah remained calm and collected. When the committee finally announced the company's decision, Hannah regained the position she had been promoted to previously.

Today, Hannah believes that she has been incredibly blessed and says, "My life is a living testimony to the blessings that Spirit provides for us."

■

Another individual, Alice Branson, never knew her mother or father. She was raised by her grandmother in Ireland. Although nearly seventy years have passed since her experience, she can recall it as easily as one might recall what they had for dinner the night before. The experience happened on Good Friday, in a small Irish town, when Alice was about six or seven years old.

As she remembers, she had been talking to her grandmother about Easter and the promises of Easter goodies, which would appear on Sunday. However, when her grandmother explained the importance of Good Friday as the day when Jesus had been crucified, Alice remembers becoming very upset: "I could not understand why anyone would want to hurt Jesus, and when she told me that no one had come to help Him, I became enraged." For some reason, in her childish mind she believed that a crucifixion that had occurred nearly 2,000 years previously was about to be re-enacted on Good Friday, and Alice became convinced that "I had to do something to help Him!" She believed that if she could reach their tiny church in time, she could be the one who finally came to His aid.

The church was across a river and a valley, and the shortest path was over a rickety wooden bridge that Alice remembers "swayed like a drunken sailor." In spite of the fact that she had long been forbidden to cross it, Alice set out on her rescue mission about 10:00 a.m. that morning. Alice remembers:

I crossed the bridge undaunted and headed in the direction of the church. When I reached a heavily wooded area, I suddenly smelled the most wonderful fragrance and veered from the path to smell some wildflowers growing there. When I stooped down to smell the flowers, I could hear the sounds of water flowing as if from a waterfall. Nobody had ever told me that a waterfall was there, so I veered further into the woods, maybe twenty feet or so.

Suddenly, I was in a beautiful grotto-like setting. There was a waterfall cascading into a pool. Bluebells, primroses, buttercups and all kinds of flowers grew all around it. I knelt down to gaze into the pool of water and sniff the flowers. When I looked up to see the top of the waterfall, there stood a bare cross.

I was amazed and delighted—they hadn't gotten him yet! I knew it was the real cross—it was old and gnarled . . . I decided I would keep watch as long as I had to. It seemed like maybe fifteen minutes passed, and then I heard my grandmother's voice.

Alice turned and seemed to run right into her grandmother who appeared shocked to see her—it was as if the child had appeared out of nowhere. Her grandmother had tears in her eyes and screamed out, "Child, where have you been?" To her surprise, Alice realized that there were many others standing around her grandmother. Apparently, dozens of people from the small village had become convinced that the child had crossed the forbidden bridge, fallen in and drowned in the waters below. Her grandmother exclaimed, "We have been looking for you for hours!" Alice was surprised to learn that it was 7:00 p.m. at night and the sun was setting.

When Alice tried to insist that she had just seen a grotto, a cross and a waterfall, one of the young girls in the group said that she was crazy. However, Alice would not relent, and she forced her grandmother to follow her back into the woods. After a long search it became clear to Alice that "there was no grotto, no waterfall, no wildflowers in bloom and no cross."

The young girl remained convinced that her story was not her imagination. However, a few days later when the village priest arrived wanting to talk to her about the experience, her grandmother shooed him away and told Alice "to never speak about my experience with anyone since they wouldn't understand."

Years later, while Alice was having a psychic reading from a talented intuitive, without being told of what had occurred, the psychic described her experience and stated that the reason her grandmother and the searchers seemed so shocked to see her was that she had literally "appeared out of nowhere." Apparently, she had somehow been transported to another dimension of time and space. The psychic suggested that the experience had been a real encounter with the Divine—one she had been able to bring to mind throughout her life whenever she felt the need. According to Alice, the experience truly helped her realize "that God is very much alive."

■

Although it may not sound like a supernatural experience to some, Anita Martinez is convinced that a Divine encounter in nature saved her and a friend from heat stroke, exhaustion and even possible death. The two of them were vacationing in La Paloma, South America—a place with miles of golden sand beaches and rolling dunes. According to Anita, they found themselves "surrounded by beautiful nature under a majestic blue sky with no sign of human life. As far as the eye can see, there are roaring waves of ocean waters and immense sand dunes constantly bathed by the intensity of the sun."

It was just such a day when Anita and her friend decided to go on an adventure—exploring what lay beyond the dunes bordering the beach and the ocean. They left the familiarity of the beach and began climbing the dunes in pursuit of a lagoon they had heard about.

Even in the early morning the sun was hot and no clouds appeared in the overhead sky. With neither wearing a hat nor carrying any water of any kind, the two continued their journey. The excitement of their adventure kept them moving over the dunes, ignoring both the heat and the difficulty of walking over endless stretches of shifting sands that fell back into place only a moment after footsteps had marked the path.

The heat of the sun beat down upon their bodies. When they finally grew tired, they paused a while to rest, but there was no shade and no water to quench their thirst. They briefly joked about the foolishness of being on such an adventure without the proper equipment and both wondered aloud how much further they were from the rumored lagoon. Because the lagoon was still not in sight, each agreed that they would journey only for a while longer before deciding to head back. When they finally continued on their way, they were shocked to see what finally greeted their eyes—on all sides they were surrounded by sand. As far as they could see there was only sand. It became immediately clear that they were lost. There was no way to tell from which way they had come or where they had been heading.

At first Anita tried to get them to retrace their footsteps, but the shifting sand soon made it clear that there was no way they could follow the way they had come. They tried to discern their bearings from the sun, but that approach proved fruitless. Not knowing what else to do, they began walking.

Perhaps it was due to the heat of the afternoon sun or perhaps their own anxiety over being lost, but their steps became more and more difficult. The sun began scorching their bodies, and their breathing became heavy and hard. All conversation between the two stopped as if it took every ounce of energy just to continue. When it seemed as though they had walked for a very long time, Anita began to grow afraid.

Suddenly, her friend seemed on the verge of tears: "What are we going to do?"

It was then that Anita looked once again to the sky to see the location of the sun. Instead, she immediately saw two seagulls flying overhead. As the birds flew by and continued off into the distance, Anita thought nothing of it. However, a moment later the birds circled back until they were once again flying overhead.

Anita pointed to the sky, "Look!" The birds flew past, and just as it seemed they were about to disappear into the distance, the two birds circled back again. "I think they want us to follow." Not having any other direction in mind, the two young women walked in the direction of the birds.

Repeatedly the birds flew overhead, and just when it seemed they were about to disappear from sight, the two seagulls circled back to make certain Anita and her friend were following. After a long while, the two young women finally spotted the water of the ocean, and with the appearance of the ocean, Anita says, "the seagulls showed us for the last time what direction we were supposed to be heading before flying away and disappearing somewhere in the sky.

Anita has no doubt that the two seagulls were Divine messengers sent to save them from a very dangerous situation. She adds:

Many people think that encounters with the Divine have to be supernatural, dramatic or somehow miraculous. I have learned, however, that we constantly have encounters with the Divine in every aspect of our lives—physically, mentally and spiritually. If we are open to looking for God in all things, we will find Him because in a very real sense, God is a part of us and we are a part of Him.

■

A simple encounter with God's presence in nature has served to fortify Gertrude Doronzo for over sixty years, enabling her to work through a variety of challenging experiences. The experience caused Gertrude to realize that even during life's darkest moments, "I was never really alone." Today, she is the retired mother of three children and seven grandchildren. Widowed during her fifties, she believes her husband's untimely death came as a result of several failed business ventures due to untrustworthy employees, repeated robberies, the underhanded business dealings of others and even arson: "All of these incidents and many others helped my husband into an early grave."

As a child, Gertrude's parents separated when she was three, and shortly thereafter her mother was diagnosed with tuberculosis. For years, her mother was in and out of hospitals and sanitariums and always seemed frail. Gertrude's grandmother ran a boarding house in the Catskill Mountains of New York, and it was there that Gertrude was sent as a child and teenager to spend each and every summer. Rather than seeing it as a hardship, she says, "I loved every minute of my time there. As a teenager I worked there as a waitress, and after supper, when the dining room was cleaned and set up for the following day's breakfast, I would go for a walk or just sit on the lawn facing Hunter Mountain." It was during one of those evenings that Gertrude experienced a Presence she has never forgotten:

> I remember that I was sitting there being very quiet. There was complete silence around me—even the insects were still. I was watching the setting sun, and it seemed much more fascinating than I had ever noticed before. I became very focused on what I was witnessing.
>
> The sky above the mountain suddenly seemed to be glowing with a rosy-orange hue. At the same time, the color of the mountain slowly

began to change from purple to indigo. I felt something well up inside of me, and as the sun set, I saw a golden light, an aura, surrounding the mountain and the sky. It's hard to explain, but in that moment I felt the presence of the Creator.

All at once, I felt a deep yearning, and the presence of love filled my entire being. Never before or since have I felt such tremendous love. My eyes began to swell with tears—even now, sixty years later, my eyes begin to tear just thinking about the experience. I just let the tears fall and basked in the presence of God. I had no doubt that I had met Him in the beauty of a sunset.

Never again would Gertrude have the experience, but it was something she frequently brought to mind when she became depressed, worried or uncertain about her life or her direction. She believes the experience "sustained me throughout my life." When asked what about the encounter has meant the most to her, Gertrude says simply, "I have never been alone."

■

Another brief encounter occurred at a young age to Abigail Richards when she was about twelve or thirteen years old. Raised in the Greek Orthodox Church and visiting relatives in a small Greek village one summer, Abigail recalls an experience that would forever confirm for her the existence of God.

On the day of her encounter, the entire family had arisen early to pick grapes from the hillside. Abigail had fallen behind the others and stopped to watch the horizon. Thinking back on the experience, Abigail recalls:

As I remember, I felt in awe of the beauty I saw before my eyes. Suddenly, I saw a gigantic hand in the sky—the hand of God pointing in the direction of the sun. It was not my imagination. I was speechless; it was like the whole Universe stood still. I could see God's hand all the way up to the wrist. I watched—I don't remember for how many seconds—and then it disappeared.

Later, Abigail told her mother, father and sisters what she had witnessed. Her father brushed it off as a childish imagination, but her sisters and mother knew her and knew that she was telling the truth. "I know what I saw!" Abigail states firmly.

When asked why she thinks the experience happened, Abigail says, "I think God wanted me to have this experience to help me in my moments of doubting Him. After this, how could I not believe that He existed? Often, I have thanked God for allowing me to see what I saw."

■

Delbert Olson has been a farmer for most of his life. Convinced of the reality of finding God in everyday events, Delbert says positively, "It may seem like a simplistic Sunday school kind of answer, but I know that many of us can find God in nature." An experience with meditation led to an encounter with "the awareness of God's oneness" that Delbert will never forget.

In brief, the encounter occurred because a friend of his who had gone away and become a psychologist and later a professor at a large university had returned for a visit. It was during his visit to the farm when Delbert mentioned his attempts at meditation. Delbert describes how his friend then planted a seed:

> I have quite a number of chickens on the farm. We had been walking around the henhouse inspecting the chickens. Now I don't know if you know this, but a chicken hatching an egg will just sit there for about three weeks waiting for that egg to hatch. She'll get off of the egg only for very brief moments of time to get a drink or to get something to eat. For the most part, she just sits there and waits.
>
> Just about the time we were looking at the chickens, I mentioned my attempts at meditation. My friend said that there was a Chinese description of meditating with a sense of expectancy, "like a chicken waiting for her eggs to hatch." Because of that remark, I decided to meditate with the chickens.

Delbert waited until one of his chickens had laid a fresh egg and then went out to the henhouse every morning to meditate with that chicken.

For three weeks, meditation in the henhouse became an important part of his routine. At first the chicken didn't know what to think, but after a few days Delbert's presence seemed almost welcome. Delbert admits, "I felt a bond with that chicken that's hard to explain—hard at least to put into words."

As the days passed, Delbert began to feel like he belonged to the process of hatching that egg. During meditation, he would watch the chicken with his eyes three-quarters closed; the chicken watched him fully alert. It was about three weeks later during his morning meditation when he heard the sounds of the egg beginning to crack:

> I have seen an egg hatch countless times before, but I had never before felt what I felt that day. As the egg began to hatch, I was so emotionally connected to the process that my eyes began to tear. I felt such a connection to the oneness of the universe at that moment. I have never felt anything like it before or since. It's hard to explain, but I was a part of that whole going on. Who knows what had happened during those three weeks, but I know firsthand that the God of oneness can become very clear to us if we can find a way to open ourselves up to that.

■

An experience with the Divine in nature also happened to Kathy Winstead when she was a thirty-year-old nurse and mother of two children. Feeling trapped in a marriage with a husband who seemed to find great joy in afflicting her with mental cruelty and continuous remarks questioning her abilities as a wife and mother, Kathy felt that "for the sake of the children" she needed to remain in the marriage. Insecure and frightened, she was convinced that there was something she was supposed to be learning in her relationship with her husband.

A student of reincarnation, sometimes Kathy couldn't help but feel "victimized" by what she regarded as her own personal karma. When she discovered that her husband was having an affair, it made the situation even worse. Kathy withdrew into herself and tried to deal with the experience as best she could. At times the stress and the emotional turmoil were nearly impossible to deal with. Sometimes going into work and dealing with the needs of far too many patients seemed easier to cope with than her life at home.

It was shortly after discovering her husband's infidelity that Kathy felt the Presence of the Divine. Even now, Kathy admits she was surprised that the experience occurred while she was, "in all places, outside of the house doing yard work!" Her husband and two children were also in the yard playing. Kathy describes the experience as follows:

I was working in my small garden and was lifting the shovel to turn over a pile of earth. I had been under a great deal of stress and was doing the yard work to relax—it also needed to be done. Suddenly, I experienced complete and total stillness:

It was as if everything became frozen in place. I could hear no sound and see no movement around me. There in the garden I felt totally connected with the entire Universe. I felt a powerful oneness with God. My entire being resonated with the wonder and joy of Life.

All at once I had the awesome realization that I was, and am, united with all that there is—all humanity, all animate and inanimate objects. I felt the presence of this Life flowing through the sky, the trees, the yard—everything around me. I became aware of the fact that this same Life force flowed through me. In those moments I knew with absolute certainty that I was not alone and that the Divine had an ongoing place in our lives.

After the experience, Kathy found that she had the strength to do what she needed to do. She was able to follow through on a divorce and to realize that she had allowed herself to continually be victimized by the relationship. She claims that in spite of divorcing her husband, she was able to begin practicing unconditional love toward him. Still a student of reincarnation, Kathy states that even with each lifetime, we are not fated to simply go through the motions: "We continually create our own reality." Even now, her encounter with the Divine continues to affect her:

The experience has sustained me through many dark nights of the soul. An inner calmness and the sense of a Divine presence have enabled me to endure and to find that place of center . . . I have truly learned to let go and to let God. I have learned to look within myself for the strength, will and understanding I need to sustain my soul. I have learned that true happiness and contentment must originate from the God-self within. As a result, I work daily at trying to stay centered, at focusing on my Divine nature and at trying to listen to my Higher Self and commune with the Divine.

7

Divine Encounters and the Death Experience

That all nations should become one in faith and all men as brothers; that the bonds of affection and unity between the sons of men should be strengthened; that diversity of religion should cease, and differences of race be annulled . . . These strifes and this bloodshed and discord must cease, and all men be as one kindred and one family . . .

Bahá'u'lláh, Bahá'I Faith
Religious Unity, 117-118

Shanti Devi was born in Delhi, India, in 1926, and from the age of three claimed to recall a previous life she had lived in Mathura, a town less than 100 miles away. As soon as she could speak, she began talking about her memories of her husband, some of the routines that had been a part of her life, her ancestry and social status and various other details including the fact that she had once given birth to a son. At first Shanti's parents thought the girl's statements were simply due to an active imagination, but Shanti's "memories" persisted.

Shanti told her parents that she did not feel as though the place where she lived was really her home—she had another home, a husband and a child. She also said that her husband had a cloth shop, that he was fair in appearance, wore reading glasses and had a wart on his left cheek. She frequently used expressions and dialectic words that were unknown to her family or to the village in which she lived. She claimed to be of a social caste different from her family's and was familiar with the customs, diet and habits of that other caste. For years, her parents tried to get her to forget her story. They had no interest in investigating her claims or taking her to the town where she said she once lived. Shanti even gave a detailed account of her death following childbirth, amazing the local doctor with her knowledge of childbirth and surgical procedures.

Until the age of eight or nine, she refused to say the name of her husband—a fact that is not so surprising when it is realized that it is customary for a woman in India not to mention the name of her husband. One day, however, a relative promised her that if she told him the name of her husband, she would be taken to the town to meet him. When Shanti finally whispered the name "Pandit Kedarnath Chaube," the relative wrote a letter to the town of Mathura and discovered that such an individual actually existed. Kedarnath himself would confirm many of the details about his deceased wife—details that Shanti had frequently described since she had been old enough to speak. As a result, Kedarnath eventually made a trip to Delhi to see the young girl himself. He was accompanied by his new wife and his son from his previous wife, who was a year older than Shanti. In order to question the girl's legitimacy, Kedarnath was introduced as the older brother of her former husband. Shanti saw through the deception immediately:

> Shanti said in a low firm voice, "No, he is not my husband's brother. He is my husband himself." Then she addressed her mother, "Didn't I tell you that he is fair and he has a wart on the left side cheek near his ear?"
>
> She then asked her mother to prepare meals for the guests. When the mother asked what she should prepare, she said that he was fond of stuffed potato parathas and pumpkin squash. Kedarnath was dumbfounded as these were his favorite dishes. Then Kedarnath asked whether she could tell them anything unusual to establish full faith in her. Shanti replied, "Yes, there is a well in the courtyard of our house, where I used to take my bath."
>
> Rawat, 19–20

Later, Shanti told Kedarnath intimate and even sexual details of their life together. So detailed were her accounts of her life as the wife of Kedarnath of Mathura, by the end of his visit Kedarnath announced that he was fully convinced Shanti was his wife reborn. After the meeting, Shanti's story came to the attention of others, including the media.

When Mahatma Gandhi heard of the girl's story, he appointed a committee of fifteen prominent individuals to study the case. Eventually, Shanti and the committee of investigators and researchers would journey to the town of Mathura. She accurately described the changes that had taken place in her village since her death. While there, the group even tried to mislead Shanti and confuse her, but Shanti could not be shaken. Shanti led the committee to her former house, pointed out a number of individuals she had known previously, including her former father-in-law. Over and over again, she was able to correctly answer questions about the former woman's life and habits. The former woman had been named "Lugdi" and had died on October 4, 1925. Shanti Devi was born one year, two months and seven days later, on December 11, 1926. By the time Shanti and the committee visited the town of Mathura, she was only ten years old. The details of her story, her confirmed memories, and the multiple investigations to examine her claims are truly amazing.

It wouldn't be until the end of the 1950s that Shanti Devi's life and experience came to the attention of the Western world through the activities of Swedish author Sture Lonnerstrand of Stockholm. An award-winning journalist, Lonnerstrand had originally intended to prove the Shanti Devi story a "fraud," but he eventually became convinced of the tale's legitimacy. After his own investigations, questioning Shanti, family members and individuals who had been part of Gandhi's committee of fifteen, he wrote a series of articles about Shanti, which were eventually published into nine languages. In time, her story would become known by a diverse group of researchers and reincarnation enthusiasts, including Manly Palmer Hall and Dr. Ian Stevenson. A few years before her death, Lonnerstrand would compile Shanti's story and his experiences with her in *I Have Lived Before,* first published in Sweden in 1994 and translated into English in 1998, the year after her death. Because of the accuracy, details and verification that became a part of her story, the case of Shanti Devi has been called "the most known and the most well-documented case of reincarnation in the world in modern times." (Lonnerstrand, 126)

In addition to her past-life memories, Shanti also claimed to recall an amazing experience with the Divine in between lifetimes that inspired her throughout her life as Shanti Devi. During a public lecture in 1993, psychologist, minister and author Dr. Herbert Bruce Puryear told a church congregation of his experience meeting Shanti Devi. According to Dr. Puryear, she was a woman who claimed to come into this life remembering a specific purpose for which she had been born. It was a purpose that had been given to her during a personal encounter with the Divine:

> There is a woman named Shanti Devi . . . Shanti Devi . . . began to remember a past life . . . she would talk about the details. She remembered the name of her husband. She remembered the town where she lived. She could speak in the dialect of that village . . . When she visited that village, she could identify her former husband . . . she calls him by name . . . she takes him to where they lived. The details are amazing . . . now here's what I want to share with you. In India, a group of us visited Shanti Devi, and we talked with her about her memory of the past life and she said,
>
> "That is nothing. That memory of that past life is nothing! What I want to tell you about is what I remember in my in-between spirit plane experiences. I was taken before the Lord himself."
>
> She called him the Lord Krishna. A Christian would probably call him the Lord Christ, but she was taken before the Throne, and she had this memory of this assignment, and she was told, "I want you to go back and do a work."
>
> Shanti Devi . . . is going about a work, and she remembers her assignment of that work while she was in the spirit plane . . . she came in to do a great work. Puryear, Ye Must Be Born Again

What is that work? According to Lonnerstrand, her biographer, "Throughout her whole life she has abstained from personal financial gain in spreading the message about her experiences. She considers it to be her natural duty, her true calling to inform people of the law of karma and reincarnation . . . " (Lonnerstrand, 131)

More than thirty years after Lonnerstrand first broke her story to the Western world, he returned to find a woman who was well known and still extremely active with her work of teaching. During their reunion, the following conversation ensued between them:

> "Do you still believe as strongly in Krishna as you used to?"
> "Naturally, I see him as a blaze of light."
> "Are you interested in Christianity?"
> "Yes, and Islam and Parsism [Zoroastrianism] as well. I teach Sanskrit which, for Hindus, is both a religion and a philosophy. I teach mostly philosophy, as it's the most important thing for us all."
> "I'm only interested in the truth," says Shanti Devi. "The truth which unites all religions and which leads us to God."
>
> Lonnerstrand, 121

In addition to her experience with the Divine and her desire to teach others the fact that God presents Himself or Herself through whatever truth we may best be able to understand, the case of Shanti Devi is very significant. For almost sixty years it was one of the most thoroughly investigated and researched cases of reincarnation, studied by literally hundreds of researchers, critics, scholars, and individuals of world-renown. No one was ever able to prove that Shanti Devi's experiences were anything less than a valid memory of the past. Her experience meeting the Divine would inspire her for the rest of her life.

■

A contemporary story of a Divine encounter is told by Reena Sharp. Reena is a sixty-three-year-old retired schoolteacher working on a Ph.D. in holism. Since retirement she has taught adult education in the subjects of personal empowerment, holistic health, Reiki, intuition and spirituality. She is happy, confident, involved in a wonderful relationship and grateful for her strong faith and her lifetime of experiences. They are experiences that have not been easy, but Reena believes they have been instrumental in helping her to become the person she is today.

Reena was born into a very dysfunctional family. Her mother was a paranoid schizophrenic, and her father was physically abusive. Her childhood memories include watching many horrific fights between her parents, experiencing the pain of being physically abused repeatedly and having to undergo incest. Even when her parents finally divorced, her mother married a second husband who was every bit as harsh and physically abusive as her birth father. Growing up, Reena says she survived by "completely going into a shell," where she felt that she had some sense of protection from the outside world.

When she was old enough to marry, Reena married a husband who was abusive, as well as mentally ill. It would be years until she realized that children who experience abuse often marry abusive spouses. In time, her harsh relationship with her husband would lead to her becoming addicted to both Valium and alcohol. Reena states that she "began going downhill even faster." Somehow she survived the years of physical abuse from her husband and her own addictions, as well as a suicide attempt. Finally, she was able to get some help in the form of Alcoholics Anonymous. Reena states confidently, "It is the greatest 'how to' spiritual group that there is. It enabled me to dig out all of the layers of fear and falsehood that were hiding God's love."

In time, she overcame addiction, codependency and her personal insecurities. She believes that in addition to A.A., a new way of thinking enabled her to move beyond her troubled past. Afterwards, she could no longer blame anyone else for her life's problems and experiences. When asked to describe what she did to change her life, Reena says this:

> I think that one of the essential first steps was learning to look at myself and not blame anyone else. I also had to take an honest appraisal of my fears, my regrets and my motives. I had to begin thinking and living in a new way. I had to work with prayer and meditation and constantly raise my consciousness to a new and healthier perspective.

The results have stood the test of time. More than twenty years of sobriety and personal healing have passed. Since that time, she has worked as a teacher, a writer, a counselor and a radio talk show host. She sees herself primarily as a teacher, teaching individuals how they can improve their own lives and become healthier—physically, mentally and spiritually—in the process. She knows firsthand how an individual can move beyond the past and live "in the now." She also believes that one of her gifts is enabling individuals to remove the blocks that prevent them from feeling God's abundant love.

In terms of her personal encounter with the Divine, Reena cites many experiences on her own road to healing, including her experiences at A.A. and her experiences in spiritual growth and support groups. However, perhaps the most amazing experience she remembers is a memory that came to her in the midst of her healing process. It is a memory that sounds similar to the experience of Shanti Devi. According to Reena, "I remembered being deceased, just prior to being born into my life as Reena. It's hard to put the experience into words, but I know it was a valid memory of my existence between earthly lives." Reena continues:

I remembered being between earthly lives. I was in the presence of God, or at least the awareness of God. I asked God if I could go down and help the people who were suffering. I was aware of so much pain and misery, and it really bothered me that so many were chained to their lack of awareness and their fear. There were so many who lacked love. It was a love they so desperately wanted, but they did not know where to look for it. I told God that this is what I wanted to help heal.

I remember being told that I could go to help, as I desired, but the best way I could do this would be to experience the problems firsthand. I needed to work through these issues and recover on my own. By approaching those who needed help in this manner, others would be able to hear what I said, they could see that these things might be overcome and I could truly provide an example to them.

I remember being hesitant and even arguing. I did not want to experience such a depth of agony and pain. Finally, because I felt such a need to help, I decided to do it anyway. I descended into an experience of living with a mentally ill family and experienced incest, my own addictions, violence and codependency. I experienced an abusive marriage. I experienced not being loved. I became a victim to the very things I had hoped to heal.

I remember being in God's presence.

As amazing as Reena's story may sound, she points out that her life and her experiences since sobriety are proof enough that her story must be real. In truth, her harsh background and her own healing process have enabled her to help others who have experienced many of the same things. She believes that she has finally found her own sense of wholeness and she has been able to share that wholeness with others. By example she has enabled individuals to remove resentment, fear and a multitude of damaging behavior from their lives.

Reena still considers herself a teacher first, but her subject matter has broadened beyond the topics you might find in school: "Today, I teach individuals how to move beyond their life challenges, how to become all they were meant to be and how to grow spiritually. I teach individuals that we are truly His children. I try to teach people that down deep in all of us, you will find God."

■

Elizabeth Richey tells the story of having been very sick—so sick, in fact, that there was a time when it was believed she was going to die. At first she thought she simply had a bad case of the flu. One moment she found herself shivering with chills, and a moment later she was sweating with an extremely high fever. Her husband, Andy, tried to get her to go to the doctor, but she had a stubborn streak and insisted on nursing her illness with over-the-counter medication. However, her breathing became worse, and when she became cold, "there weren't enough blankets in the house to make me feel warm." When she started to sweat, she would soak several layers of towels simply trying to stay dry. When her breathing became even more difficult, Andy insisted, "We're going to the hospital." The couple called Andy's mother, Louise, to take care of their children.

Elizabeth was briefly examined at the hospital. She insisted she needed to be at home, but Andy was told by the doctor, "We're admitting your wife immediately . . . she's not going anywhere." Several rounds of testing led to a diagnosis. Andy was informed that his wife appeared to have one of the rarest and most dangerous forms of pneumonia: "staphylococcal pneumonia." When he asked about his wife's prognosis and the seriousness of the illness, he was horrified when one of the doctors finally admitted, "This type of pneumonia is very rare and very serious . . . it can have a death rate of fifteen to thirty percent."

Even after being hospitalized, Elizabeth seemed to grow worse. She became delirious and was frequently drifting in and out of consciousness. She was put in an oxygen tent, and all Andy could do was helplessly sit by her side and touch one of her legs or an arm under the blanket. Elizabeth often cried out in pain, and her breathing sounded as if it were filled with congestion. The doctors informed him that his wife's breathing was becoming harsher due to the fact that bacteria had formed somewhere in her lungs and was producing an abscess. On the third day in the hospital, his wife was given a chest tube to help drain the pus that was building up in her lungs.

Not knowing whether or not his wife was going to survive, the hospital let Andy have a bed in her room to stay by her side. Mostly delirious, when his wife was conscious, she cried out in pain from the pressure in her chest and from the tube between her ribs. Later, Elizabeth told of an experience she had while Andy was sitting next to her in the hospital:

I remember passing out several times. I was in so much pain that I just wanted it to end. I was ready to give up and die just to get out of the pain. One day, after a particularly painful morning, I felt myself float out of my body. I looked down and could see myself sitting under the oxygen tent, and I could see Andy sitting next to me. I felt more like I an observer than a participant in what was going on below me.

All at once I felt myself moving—like the wind was rushing past me and I was moving along with it. Suddenly, I was surrounded by a circular tunnel, and straight ahead I could see the most beautiful light. As I moved toward the light, I became aware of the fact that I couldn't feel any pain. My body didn't hurt anymore. It was at that point that I wondered inside my head, "I wonder if I'm really dead?"

When I got to the end of the tunnel, I could see the shadowy forms of people off to the sides, but the light in front of me is what drew my attention. The light was brilliant. It was so bright that you would have thought that you would have to squint your eyes, but the light didn't hurt at all. When my gaze stopped and really looked at the light to see what it was, it was then that a bright figure walked out of it. I knew the figure was Jesus.

Jesus didn't speak, but I somehow "heard" words inside of my head, "It's not your time." I also felt total acceptance and unconditional love emanating from him. Even though I'm not really a churchgoer, it didn't really matter. We always say my mother-in-law is the religious one in the family, but I could feel that Jesus knew and loved *me* regardless! I was totally accepted and loved. I felt in the presence of such unconditional love that I really wanted to stay.

All at once, Jesus seemed to send the image of Andy into my head. I could see Andy sitting next to me in the hospital room. As soon as I started thinking about Andy, I felt myself getting pulled back from Jesus, from the light and from the people that had been standing at the end of the tunnel. At some point, I became conscious of feeling pain again, and a moment later I know I passed out. That's all I remember.

Meanwhile, while the experience was occurring to Elizabeth, Andy says that he was "praying and crying." He found himself crying real tears and praying for his wife's recovery, which did not appear hopeful. He thought of his children and the fact that they would not have a mother. He felt very depressed and worried. All at once, while praying, he became conscious of seeing the face of his own mother, deep in prayer, back at the house. Andy is convinced: "There's no mistaking what I saw." Just seeing his mother's face seemed to give him a great deal of comfort. Interestingly enough, when Andy would later mention his experience to his mother, she seemed quite surprised. As near as they could tell, apparently at the very moment his experience was occurring, Louise was deep in prayer herself, praying for Elizabeth and Andy.

After Elizabeth's Near Death Experience, she began a slow recovery. In all, she would spend five weeks in the hospital and lose nearly thirty pounds. Even now, she has no doubt that she saw Jesus or that the experience was real. It remains very vivid and real to her—an experience with the Divine that literally occurred between the moments of life and death.

■

Frannie Vedder does not claim to have any kind of special psychic ability, nor does she think that her experience is something that will necessarily be repeated. In her own words, "I think my experience was simply because conditions were optimal at that time and that place." Today, Frannie is a woman in her fifties, and her experience occurred nearly three decades in the past, but it is something that she will never forget: "After that experience, there was never a doubt in my mind that we survive physical death. It was right there in front of me—it would be ludicrous for me to believe otherwise."

One day when Frannie was alone in her apartment building, she found herself doodling and writing a series of letters on a notepaper, simply passing the time. After a moment, the paper appeared to be filled with the words *lance* and *hill* written over and over again. As soon as Frannie saw what she was doing, she felt goose bumps and chills cover her entire body. Convinced she was scaring herself, Frannie put the piece of paper down.

Shortly thereafter, one of her friends in the apartment building called, and Frannie eventually mentioned her experience, laughing at her wild imagination. There was a long silence on the phone before her friend spoke:

"Lance Hill was my grandfather," she said softly. "He died two years ago."

Shocked at the thought that a deceased individual had somehow contacted her, Frannie decided that she needed further proof. After she had hung up the phone, she closed her eyes and thought, "If only I could see what this person looked like."

No sooner had the thought been formed than a man's face began to appear in her mind's eye. She saw what looked like a negative—a transparent picture in reverse composed of black, white and shades of gray. The man also had a glow of light gently pulsating around his head. Frannie is certain:

It was not a dream. I knew without a doubt that what I was seeing was real. I'd never experienced it before. He had dark piercing eyes, two deep wrinkles on each side of his nose and a receding hairline. He just stared straight back at me and seemed worried or upset about something. I also started to sense an excruciating pain in my left knee.

All at once Frannie opened her eyes—somehow convinced she had seen "the other side." So as not to lose her impressions, she quickly sketched the face that had just appeared to her. She called her friend and related the experience. Her friend stated that Lance Hill had died of cancer but she knew absolutely nothing about whether or not he had suffered from knee pain.

The next day, her friend brought her Grandmother, Lance's widow, to the door along with the family photo album. There was no question among any of the three women—Frannie's drawing was a perfect likeness of Lance Hill. During the same conversation, her friend's grandmother also confirmed that toward the end of his life Lance had suffered from terrible bursitis in his left knee.

Later that day, Frannie's friend returned in private and said that she was having an extramarital affair and she felt certain that her grandfather was trying to reach her with a warning. Her friend needed no further encouragement to break off the affair. The experience enabled the friend to "get her life back in order." Frannie is convinced that somehow she was able to act as a bridge between the living and the deceased. The experience also convinced her that "there is much more to life and what lies beyond than most people have ever imagined."

■

In another example, Polly Dale was thirty-nine years old when her mother died. Extremely close to her mother, as well as her younger sister, Aggie, Polly's biggest regret was that her mother had not lived long enough to attend Aggie's wedding. Their mother had died in February of pulmonary fibrosis, and Aggie's wedding was scheduled for May. Polly recalls, "My mother's one wish was that she would be able to live long enough to see my sister married." Regrettably, the older woman just did not have the strength to last until the wedding.

Polly was heartbroken after her mother's death. She dealt with her sadness and coped as best as she could be praying, meditating and writing in her journal as a means of dealing with the grief process: "I would also draw pictures of how I felt and write down my thoughts about feeling abandoned and lonely and missing my mother so much that it physically hurt. I would pray daily for relief and guidance and then meditate."

She missed everything about her mother—their conversations, their laughs, just having someone to call at some point in the day. Her mother had been a presence she could always rely upon, and now she was gone. Polly found that little things constantly reminded her of her mother. Something might happen during the course of Polly's daily activities, and she would catch herself thinking that she wanted to call her mother simply to talk about it. Some discussion of Aggie's pending wedding might come up, and thoughts would turn to her mother. Her mother had also been an avid collector of butterflies—the woman often wore silk ones in her hair or sent greeting cards that featured butterflies. Many times during the week, Polly would see a picture or image of a butterfly and think about her mother. Her grief continued for about three weeks, and then one day Polly had a vision of her mom.

After meditating for a while, Polly suddenly saw her mother appear before her bathed in a beautiful light. Rather than being sickly and frail, however, her mother seemed robust, healthy and much younger. Her mother also had something to show her. According to the notation in Polly's journal, "When I lifted my eyes for a brief instant, I had a very clear vision of a butterfly, and I heard my mother's voice say, 'This is my gift to you.'" After that experience, Polly no longer felt sad or depressed. Instead, she felt a profound sense of inner peace. In fact, the awareness of her mother's presence continued:

I must tell you, I continued to have a strong sense that she was still very near. At times, I had such a strong sense of her that it seemed like I could smell her or feel her in my soul. A few times I wondered if I was going off the deep end, but then I began to believe that my mother had decided to stay around at least until my sister's wedding. I began to feel a great deal of comfort whenever I sensed that mother was close by.

During my sister's wedding ceremony and Mass, I just knew that mother was there—both physically and emotionally. I could feel her as if she was standing right next to me. At one point I even felt something brush my hair, and then I heard my mother whisper in my ear: "I am so proud of you."

Later then night, after my husband had gone to bed and I was praying and meditating, I heard her voice again: "I am so proud of you and Aggie . . . you both made me very happy."

All at once I could see my mother standing in the most unbelievable pure white light. She turned and seemed to move deeper and deeper into the light, until she and the light began to fade. After a few moments, the light and my mother were totally gone, and I was left alone in the room. I knew in that instant that her spirit had left the earth completely and that she had moved on to higher realms of consciousness.

Today, Polly looks back on the experience "as a gift." Although she no longer feels her mother's presence, she feels forever changed by the experience. In addition to helping her overcome her grief, she no longer has to wonder about the abstract reality of an afterlife: "Before, I used to think in terms of life, death and the hereafter. Now I know that life and death are simply part of a continuum process."

■

Amy Malloy is a fifty-year-old licensed clinical social worker with a practice in individual and family therapy. She is also an educator and a lifelong social activist. According to Amy, one of the most important relationships she ever experienced in life was with her dog, Terry, a Tibetan terrier. Her close relationship with the terrier would become one of the most moving spiritual encounters of her entire life. According to Amy, her connection with Terry seemed to begin the moment she first saw the puppy:

My encounter with the Divine began the moment Terry entered my life, the moment I was overcome with a burning fire of recognition—with a love that reached beyond the boundaries of space and time. Not only was there a recognition of her spirit as one that was familiar from another time or space but she radiated such purity, holiness, peacefulness and love that my heart instantly knew that I was in the presence of a divine being.

While I do believe that every living being from all kingdoms—earth, animal, human, etc.—is part of the Divine, this encounter with Terry was beyond anything that I had ever experienced before.

Amy acquired her dog at a time in life when she was in the midst of confusion and despair. The dog would help her immeasurably. In time, Terry would change the way Amy viewed herself, the way she worked with people as a psychotherapist, and her understanding of the power of love. No ordinary dog, the magnetism Terry put forth eventually enabled the terrier to place in the All-American Dog Pageant. The dog would also be named "Pet with the Most Character" at a New York City event, be awarded a pet modeling contract, and land the role of Sandy in a production of the musical *Annie*.

As the years passed, Amy's bond with Terry only grew. At one point in Amy's life her adrenal system shut down, causing painful oozing blisters on her face, arms and hands. The pain was excruciating, as if her entire body were on fire. Describing the condition and how the dog helped her, Amy says this:

Most days I could not sit, walk or move without feeling unbearable pain. The sensation was as if someone had poured acid on my body and thrown a match on me. My skin felt as if it was on fire, and I wanted to tear it off. I could not be touched, nor could I have clothing touch these areas of my body. I lay with ice packs on my body, but while that cooled my body temperature down, it often irritated my skin even further.

The ONLY relief I got was when Terry would gently and methodically lick my skin and sores for hours at a time. It was the only touch that I could tolerate. Her touch soothed me from the inside out. When I would begin to tear at my skin, Terry was there to push my hand away and begin her healing ritual. She gave and gave with devotion and love. When I told my medical doctors what was happening, they conferred that animal saliva was purer than the saliva of a human and agreed that Terry's actions had great healing qualities.

Even after Amy was finally healed of her condition, Terry remained a constant companion. The dog attended walkathons and peace rallies, often wearing a shirt that read "Paws for Peace" or "Canines for Social Responsibility." She became a favorite of activists and college students and countless individuals looking for a photo opportunity. She became a tool for opening people's hearts, putting aside fear and bringing smiles to those who previously had none to give. For over fourteen years Terry was a central part of Amy's life and family.

When the terrier began to grow ill, it was a while before veterinarians detected the presence of a brain tumor. The diagnosis was that Terry would not live more than a couple of months. Refusing to give up, Amy worked with nutrition and exercise and love. After two months had passed, the terrier was eating better, seemed more alert, and even appeared healthier—the changes surprised even the veterinarians. When Terry continued to improve, one of the vets said, "There is no medical reason to explain why she is still alive. The only explanation has to be the power of your love for each other." However, even their bond could not keep the dog alive forever. The time came when it became clear that Terry could not last much longer. The terrier did live one year longer to the day that the veterinarian had suggested Terry couldn't last beyond a couple of months. Amy describes their last moments together, as follows:

While stroking her elegant body and snow white hair, I shared my deep love for her, how I wanted her to be at peace, and thanked her for all that she had given me in our life together. I let her know that she no longer had to take care of me, and that if she felt it was time for her to leave, then I honored her in that decision—though I would always miss her. I knew she had fought so valiantly to live and lived so graciously and peacefully. In the pit of my stomach I also knew her time was close. I prayed with her and showered her with my unfaltering love . . .

Amy meditated for a while and continued to stroke Terry's body until her dog took one final stretch, one final breath, and then passed into sleep. After her passing, Amy gently picked her up, held her close and gave her one final kiss.

As the weeks passed, Amy thought there were moments when she could smell Terry's scent nearby. On a couple of occasions, the dog's presence felt so real that Amy was convinced that the terrier was leaning up against her leg. One morning while she was out for a walk, Amy was sure that her dog was walking by her side—just as the terrier had done on hundreds of occasions. Once, while looking toward the sun, Amy felt certain she had seen Terry's face. On various occasions for nearly two years, Amy sensed that Terry was still a part of her life.

However, the day came when a friend gave Amy another terrier puppy, and within two weeks Terry would make her presence known for the final time. While going for a long walk and planning to visit Terry's grave at the end, a beautiful butterfly landed on Amy's shoulder, where it remained for hours. It was only after visiting the grave that the butterfly finally took its flight—Amy took it as a sign that Terry had decided to move on just as Amy needed to move on with her life, as well. Although even now, Amy states without hesitation, "She is forever in my heart."

■

Phyllis Norman considers herself religious, Christian and not at all prone to "idle fantasies or a vivid imagination." In the midst of an unusual experience after the death of a friend and co-worker, she couldn't help but think, "This isn't supposed to happen according to my Baptist dogma!" However, it did happen, and it is an experience that Phyllis will never forget.

The story is about a close friend and co-worker of hers named Arthur, who was also a member of her church. Arthur was one of those individuals who always seemed to have a cheery hello and a few kind words that he shared with other members of the office staff. Arthur loved his job and the other employees, and although he was sixty-five, he had no desire to retire.

Unfortunately, the company had a mandatory retirement policy. As a result, Arthur begged the company's president to allow him to stay on with the firm—there was really nothing else he wanted to do with his life. He loved being at the company—it was his whole life. According to Phyllis, "After much pleading, Arthur was given a conditional reprieve. The condition was that he had to be 100% cleared of any health problems, and then he could stay on."

In between the various warehouse buildings and the shipping dock, the company had a water fountain and coffee area that was kind of a gathering place for employees on break. The morning of Arthur's appointment with the doctor, Phyllis heard Arthur talking about his Christian beliefs with a visiting electrician, who was repairing some overhead lighting in one of the warehouses. Arthur assured him, "If I died today, I would know where I was going!" He talked about his belief in heaven and being "saved" and invited the electrician to come to their church. Not one for proselytizing, herself, Phyllis simply listened to Arthur's enthusiasm.

During lunchtime, the electrician and Arthur had apparently gathered in the break room to continue their discussion. Although Phyllis had been at her desk at the time, later she heard how Arthur had simply got up from the table to get a drink. On his way to the water fountain, he had suddenly fallen to the floor, dead from a fatal heart attack.

"I was totally shocked," Phyllis admits, "especially after having overheard Arthur earlier that same morning talking about death."

Arthur was buried, and as the days passed, the rest of the company got on with their business. Monday morning came, and Phyllis got back to her routine. In the midst of carrying purchase orders to the shipping department, she walked into the break room to get a cup of coffee. As she turned the corner, she felt herself run into something, like a wall that wasn't there:

> I had been concentrating on the order that needed expediting, so it was a complete shock when I turned the corner and WHAM! I felt myself run into something. The air felt so thick that it completely knocked my consciousness from my papers. All at once, I swear I heard Arthur's voice say "Why isn't anyone speaking to me?" I was so taken aback that I yelled out, "What?" and Arthur repeated himself: "Why isn't anyone speaking to me?" I yelled back, "You're dead!" I'm grateful that no one else was around.

Although my eyes couldn't see anything, I knew that Arthur was there. I could literally "feel" his presence and personality. I even felt him wondering why everyone had been ignoring him.

"Arthur, you're dead."

Here, the same individual who had been so positive that he knew where he was going when he died didn't even know that he was dead.

When she repeated her words, "Arthur, you're dead," Phyllis says that she felt the strangest sensation. "It was almost as if a shock wave passed through the air in front of me. It seemed like Arthur took a step back, and it felt like he looked upward toward the ceiling. All at once his presence disappeared, and the air in the room felt normal again. Arthur had finally moved on."

Although Phyllis quickly left the room, she soon felt guilty that she had been so abrupt: "Why hadn't I been gentler with him? I should have suggested that he look for the Light and someone would come help him. It must have been a real shock for him to suddenly realize that he was dead."

Phyllis is convinced that her encounter was real. She also believes that her experience simply suggested that "I still have much more to learn."

■

Another unusual account of encountering the Divine during the death experience is the story of Patty Larson. Both her background and upbringing had been very conservative—first as a child growing up in Canada and then as a certified general accountant for the Canadian government. However, Patty has encountered various life experiences that she says have served as "a wake up call" to the mysteries of the universe. One of her most unusual and profound experiences occurred at the age of sixty when she had accompanied a tour group to Egypt.

For Patty, the trip was the fulfillment of a lifelong dream. Her husband had not shared the same enthusiasm or desire to make the journey, so she had taken the trip alone, along with a metaphysical group that she had become involved with. In all, about forty individuals were on the tour. Together they toured much of Egypt, from Cairo and Giza in the north to Aswan and Abu Simbel in the south. They saw countless temples and ornate tombs, stretches of desert sand and the lush beauty of the Nile. In fact, as part of their journey, for several days Patty and her group got to sail up the Nile on a houseboat.

The trip included tours to all of the major sites, including the Cairo museum, the Great Pyramid, the Sphinx, Luxor, the Valley of the Kings, the unfinished obelisk and the Aswan High Dam. Along the way the group heard various historical and archeological lectures. They also had the opportunity to meditate together each day, have a dream discussion each morning and eat their meals together. Patty enjoyed the group bonding that occurred, and she soon became very close to an older man on the trip, "a real character named Mike McDougall, who was about eighty years old."

Just as it had been for Patty, Mike considered the trip to be the culmination of a lifelong dream. Appearing to be much younger and energetic than his eighty years, Mike brandished an Irish wit and loved to engage individuals in long conversations about his philosophy of life. It wasn't too many days after the trip had begun that Mike latched onto Patty, and the two became inseparable during the rest of their tour. Mike became her friend and mentor, according to Patty:

> About halfway through the trip I had grown quite attached to him. I even thought about making a trip with my husband to see him after the tour was over. My relationship with Mike was so close so quickly that it felt like we were simply picking up a friendship where it had been left off.

One of the highlights of the tour was scheduled to occur on the last day. The group was going to have a private meditation in the King's Chamber of the Great Pyramid at Giza, followed by a farewell dinner at the hotel. Both Patty and Mike were looking forward to the experience, and Patty hoped that the meditation in that special place would provide her with insights as to what she was supposed to be doing next in her life.

When the final day arrived, the group made the long journey up into the Pyramid and finally came together in the large room of the King's Chamber. When everyone had found a place to sit on the floor, Patty began her meditation. She describes her experience, as follows:

> While I was meditating, I had what I can only describe as "a vision." Because I had just retired from my position with the Canadian government, throughout the trip I had found myself wondering, "What am I supposed to do now?" While I was meditating, that same question came to mind and brought with it a visionary experience:
>
> I could plainly see a double row of Egyptian guards standing in front of me, waiting for something to happen. They had on gold and blue headpieces and looked very regal, but they were simply standing and waiting. I felt myself wonder what they were waiting for, but they just stood there.
>
> Every time I asked the question, "God, what am I supposed to do now with my life?" Mike came into view, and I heard him say, "You are already doing it; just be patient." Now this isn't what I wanted to hear, nor was I expecting to see Mike, so I kept on persisting. However, the experience simply kept repeating itself.

After the meditation was over, the group went back to the hotel for their final dinner and get together. Mike had offered to entertain the group with a song, so Patty volunteered to help him get dressed and ready for his performance. Mike had brought with him an Irish costume and was truly happy and proud that he was going to have the opportunity to sing to the group.

The dinner was wonderful, and afterwards Mike got up to begin his song. During the performance, Patty stood about ten feet away and watched him proudly. She admits, "Even though we had just met, I felt an uncanny attraction and closeness to him."

Although Mike was in great spirits and very energetic about his performance, shortly after he started to sing, he simply collapsed and fell to the floor. Several members of the tour ran forward and announced with horror and surprise, "He's dead!" Patty, however, was unable to move from her spot, which "is totally unlike my left-brained way of dealing with things." All at once she found that her mind had returned to the meditation she experienced earlier:

It hadn't happened because I wanted it to. Suddenly, I saw what I had seen earlier. The guards were still patiently waiting, and Mike was there, as well. All at once the scene started to change. I can't really describe how I felt or what I saw. All I can say is that the human language does not have words to adequately describe the experience:

I found myself somewhere else with Mike. It was somewhere beautiful, bright, warm and exceedingly wonderful. I looked at Mike and said sadly, "Don't go; I just found you."

He smiled, "You will be all right now. You are already on the path—just be patient."

I begged him again, "Don't go!"

He sighed quietly and smiled, "This is what I have waited for all of my life. I am going to go now . . . You need to go, too."

I knew that he meant I was supposed to return to the hotel.

All at once I found myself back in the room, still standing there. A doctor had been called in, and he had just proclaimed that Mike was dead. I carefully helped remove his outer costume and put it back into his little travel bag. Afterward, I went back to my room, without speaking to anyone. To tell the truth, I'm not sure I could have spoken even if I had wanted to.

I haven't told this story to too many people. I can't do it justice with words; part of me doesn't really know why I had the experience. Another part of me believes that Mike had been my mentor in the long ago past and we came together briefly so that he could reassure me that I was doing the right thing and that I was on the right path. I pray that's the case.

Today, through a series of experiences and choices, Patty has become the CEO of the small metaphysical organization that she originally accompanied on the tour to Egypt. Her life has completely turned around from her days as an accountant. She no longer feels the need to ask "What am I supposed to be doing?" because her work provides her with tremendous fulfillment and a sense of purpose. Looking back on the tour, she believes that she and Mike came together simply to reaffirm that she was on the right path and headed in the right direction:

To say that God has worked in mysterious ways would be putting it mildly. Sometimes I feel like I have lived two lives in one lifetime—one before, while I was walking in confusion and fog, and one now, when I have had the opportunity to walk in the light. I now meditate regularly, am active in my non-profit work and participate in many educational programs. In a real sense, I have found what I had been looking for all of my life—even when I didn't know that I had been looking for it.

Conclusion

They are not of the world, even as I am not of the world . . .
That they all may be one; as thou, Father, art in me, and I
in thee, that they also may be one in us:
that the world may believe that thou hast sent me.
And the glory which thou gavest me I have given them;
that they may be one, even as we are one . . .

The Holy Bible
John 17:16, 21-22

Friedrich Nietzche (1844–1900), the German philosopher and poet, has perhaps become most well known in today's society for writing three simple words: "God is dead." However, Nietzche's statement was not an expression of his personal opinion but rather a warning of his predicted outcome should society supplant faith and spiritual ideals for the allure of the modern world. And yet, in spite of Nietzche's concern, stories that explore the innumerable ways in which the Divine makes itself known would seem to suggest that God is very much alive.

This book grew out of my experiences traveling and speaking upon five continents. Because I often speak about contemporary spirituality and the ease of facilitating personal intuitive experiences, over the years I have often been approached by members of my audiences who wished to relate a story they "just had to tell someone." The end result was that I had repeated opportunities to hear wonderful accounts of people's experiences with God or some aspect of the Divine. Oftentimes that story was a dream, an episode of heightened awareness, a visionary encounter, or some kind of supernatural healing that seemed to defy logic while briefly touching upon a world of spiritual consciousness.

Frequently individuals began their stories with a phrase such as "You are never going to believe what I'm going to tell you" or "I hope you don't think I'm crazy." Eventually, this interaction became so common that I often countered with "There's nothing you could tell me that I haven't heard before." However, I discovered many things I had not heard before, for there seemed to be innumerable ways in which individuals became certain that they had encountered something amazing, inspiring, powerful and even holy beyond themselves. These frequent interactions led me to wonder just how common Divine encounters were in the annals of human history. To my surprise, I soon discovered that the stories I was hearing had occurred for literally thousands of years. In time, I created a simple survey exploring the possibility of Divine encounters in contemporary life that I made available to individuals who expressed an interest in telling their stories. Eventually, more than one hundred individuals would ask to participate. The survey was composed of questions that essentially asked each participant to answer the following:

- *Give a brief, general biographical history about yourself*
- *Describe your encounter with God or some aspect of the Divine*
- *Why do you think the experience happened to you?*
- *What was occurring in your life at the time of your experience?*
- *Describe your personal or spiritual belief system—especially in terms of whether or not it has changed since your personal encounter*

In spite of the fact that I had created a survey for individuals to simply fill out, I was truly surprised by how many people also wanted to verbally describe their story to me personally, rather than simply filling out the questionnaire's pages. It soon became clear that many of the participants had told very few people of their personal encounters. Some said that no one really understood (or believed) their experience. Others expressed how it seemed as if their experience had been belittled because someone close to them hadn't been as powerfully affected by the story as they had.

One woman from Florida told me, "The real experience had to live in my heart; I could never mention it for fear of being thought crazy." Another gentleman in Oklahoma described how the one experience that had meant "the most in life" was the very experience that had been labeled by his church as "the work of the devil." He went on to say that he was certain that anyone else who shared a personal encounter with the Divine would find the following attitude among most listeners: "If it fits into my personal worldview, it's part of God; if not, at best it's delusional. At worst it's demonic."

As I began collecting these experiences, it soon became evident that many stories detailed similar personal encounters, which is essentially what resulted in the various chapter headings. On a number of occasions, individuals also described the experience of feeling a presence that actually "touched" them. Since these encounters are not detailed elsewhere, I have included three of these encounters below:

■

The first is the story of a fifty-something salesman, who decided to end his sales calls early in the day because of the threat of an approaching snowstorm. He describes his experience, as follows:

I had made all my calls and was ready to go home. The drive generally took about an hour and forty-five minutes.

Although things started out perfectly well, it wasn't twenty minutes later that it seemed like I had passed into another world. It was snowing so badly that I could hardly see. It was like a curtain had suddenly fallen down, surrounding the car and everything around me with snow.

I wanted to pull off to the side of the road, but I was afraid someone coming behind me would hit me. I trudged along, just going a few miles an hour. Even with the windshield wipers on, I couldn't see a thing, just barely making out a part of the road in front of me. The snow was becoming so bad that I was the last car that made it through that section of the interstate before the state troopers closed the road to all northbound traffic.

I kept driving as best I could until the wind-chill became so strong that the windows started icing up. It was so bad that even the wipers weren't cleaning the windshield. I really started to panic. Not knowing what else to do, I pulled over and got out to wipe off the windshield with my gloves. I did as best as I could and then got back inside the car.

As soon as I got into the car, something happened. I felt a *firm hand* push down on each shoulder, taking control of my driving. I started up again and kept driving, and the snow kept falling. I don't know how it happened, but somehow I made it home. I felt the hands on my shoulders all the rest of the way. I have no doubt the Lord drove me home that day.

It took me four and a half hours to get to the house, and I walked in the door just as I heard my wife say to someone on the phone, "He'll never come home through this. He'll get a hotel and stay for another day . . . "

It turned out to be the worst snowstorm we had seen in nearly twenty years.

■

The second story is that of a grown woman who describes her experience as a child being saved from near drowning. Even today, she remains certain that her "lifeguard" was not of this world:

I grew up on the Atlantic coast and as a child loved to romp in the waves at the beach. One day, while playing in the surf at Jones Beach, I was knocked down by a big wave and could not regain my footing fast enough to avoid the next big wave, which crashed over my head. I could not breathe fast enough and began to lose consciousness as the waves tumbled me over and over. There was no terror, only a feeling of great peace, as though I were being rocked in loving arms. Then suddenly, strong arms scooped me up and out of the water. A man had apparently noticed what was happening and rescued me. He restored me to the beach and my aunts. I was little worse for wear. The funny thing was, as soon as my aunts looked up to thank him, he was gone. There was no man in sight. There was no one else on the beach. We were alone. The man had vanished as mysteriously as he had appeared.

■

The third account is from a man who describes how angry he became because someone actually had the nerve to grab him:

I am now fifty-four years old. The story happened when I was eighteen. It was a Saturday morning, and I was standing on a curb, heading from the north to the south, and waiting for the red pedestrian light to give me the go-ahead green light.

When the light changed, I placed my foot in the pedestrian zone.

Suddenly, a FIRM GRASP took my right triceps and pulled me backwards onto the curb. I was angry. Who grabbed me? How dare they!

Just then I felt an absolute "gush" of wind swoosh passed me. It was a car's gust of wind, running through the red light, right over the spot where I had stepped.

I looked around to thank the person who helped me, but no one was there. Nor was anyone walking away who might have retrieved me from the crosswalk. I stood there in awe for a few moments, realizing that a Divine crossing guard from another dimension had somehow intervened!

There is no doubt I would have been hit and made into cream of mushroom soup that day, right there on the pavement.

■

While listening to, reading and then re-reading these stories of encounters with the Divine, a number or descriptive elements and themes seemed to recur with regularity as the individuals related their experiences. Certainly some of the encounters were described as being more life changing than others, but regardless of the magnitude, most of the experiences seemed to possess a number of things in common. Even when an account seemed truly unique, it definitely contained similarities with some of the other stories that had been described by participants. Although each story did not necessarily entail each element listed below, what follows is a listing of the nine themes and descriptive elements that were repeatedly mentioned with regularity. Some accounts had many of these descriptive elements in common; others may have contained only a few.

Themes and descriptive elements most frequently cited in personal Divine encounters:

- *The experience leaves the individual forever changed*
- *The experience is often hard to describe in words; it is an experience unlike anything before or since*
- *The experience helps sustain the individual throughout the rest of his or her life*
- *The experience often expands and deepens the individual's faith*
- *The experience facilitates an understanding that there is a reason for everything; life becomes a purposeful experience*
- *There is a sense of oneness; there is a profound sense of connection with the universe, with others and with one's surroundings*
- *The experience entails the presence of a love that is indescribable*
- *There is an awareness that God has an ongoing concern for us*
- *During the experience, everything stands still—there is the absence of sound, space and time*

1) The Experience Leaves the Individual Forever Changed

Most often, individuals who have experienced a personal encounter with the Divine cite specific and lasting change that has occurred in their lives ever since the experience. In a variety of ways, the experience is credited with having been the impetus for completely changing the individual's life, as well as his or her perception, world view, beliefs or thought processes. After the experience, there is often a sense of reassessing what is truly important in life. There is also a sense that the individual's perception after the experiences has been somehow expanded or broadened. Fears and worries that were once part of the past may no longer be important. Rather than being so self-absorbed, individuals often describe how they have become more involved with other people, finding themselves trying to reach out and help others rather than being so focused on personal problems and concerns.

Other changes that are frequently mentioned as being a result of a Divine encounter might best be described as improvements in behaviors or personality transformations—things like becoming more patient, being less prone to criticism, being less judgmental, being more open to the beliefs of others, being able to overcoming fear, and being able to release guilt are all a part of this personal transformation. Finally, many participants are apt to point out how they no longer fear death because they now possess a personal awareness that death is not the end.

Some of the ways in which individuals describe these changes in themselves are as follows:

"The experience allowed me to value myself. I needed to value myself. A very cruel family fate during the Hitler regime left my mother alone, struggling with four children, barely able to survive. As a child, it seemed that everyone hated us, abused us and mistreated us. So, I thought, 'If other people do not like us, how can I like myself?' There was a time when I blamed myself for everything. The experience taught me to look inside myself and see what a beautiful person was living there inside. I needed to believe in myself. I needed to trust myself, and most of all I needed to know that I was loved so that I could love myself. This realization has enabled me to see the beautiful gifts I have that I can share with others in many ways, trying to help others cope with life. Since my experience, I feel my life is simply to serve and aid others."

"Much of my life had been lived in fear. Fear has many faces: selfishness, pride, self-centeredness, worry, greed, envy and lust. However, I have become aware of some of my lessons and challenges in this regard. I can't say that I have mastered them, but I do believe I am living more in accord with faith, love, cooperation, patience, compassion and empathy. I am living as close as I can to an ideal of the Christ Consciousness. I believe it is a process."

"At the time of my experience, I was carrying so much guilt for giving up a child for adoption. I was completely able to change that guilt into thankfulness that I had been able to bear this child in order to make another mother happy. I no longer have any guilt. I have also met my birth son, and I know his life was good and I did the right thing. It has been a tremendous healing."

"After my experience, I realized that I could start treating people with the same emotions of compassion and love that I had felt. It has changed my home life and my job. It has solidified my belief in the existence of spirit and the possibility of living a spiritual life."

"I have learned to depend on myself and not to look to others to live my life. My philosophy has also changed. I now believe that a good hug is better than any prescription and that a good laugh is often the best exercise of the day."

"I have turned from being a victim, to being in control of my life. I may not always be able to control what happens to me, but I can control how I choose to act or react. I now take responsibility for my actions. As a result, even my marriage has improved. My husband tells me that I am setting an example for him. I know I am trying to share the same love I experienced with others."

"Before, I lived life by repeatedly getting hit in the head with a baseball bat. Sometimes I was beaten down so far that no earthly power could help me up . . . but now I have learned to surrender before the bat strikes. Believe me; it has saved me from a lot of pain. I have learned to 'let go and let God.'"

"I have overcome my fear of death. I am completely reassured that death is not the end. I know that there is a world beyond what we can see that has a place for each of us. I know because I have seen it for myself. I know that God loves us all unconditionally."

"I had a good friend who died of cancer a couple of years ago. She had a long and lingering illness and was down to skin and bones when she finally passed over. About a year after she died, she came to me in a dream. At least I think it was a dream, even though I felt like I was fully awake. Anyway, she was standing in the middle of a beautiful, green, lush garden. I said, 'Lorraine, how are you?' and she responded, 'I'm fine now, but I am moving to another place.' She looked beautiful, healthy, revitalized. She said, 'Look who I found here,' and she bent down and picked up my little dog that had passed over six months before. It was then that I noticed that she had her black cat that had died, with a white dot on his nose, under her arm, as well."

"The afternoon of my husband's death from cancer, I heard him speak clearly with a great deal of emotion, 'Oh, it is so beautiful here!'"

2) The Experience Is Often Hard to Describe in Words; It Is an Experience unlike Anything Before or Since

Frequently, individuals who have experienced an encounter with the Divine state that the experience is extremely hard for them to describe in words. Many of these experiences seem to contain emotions, feelings or sensations that have no point of reference that can be easily understood by people who have not had an experience of their own. For those who have had a Divine encounter, there is often the sense that there is really nothing in the physical world to compare the encounter with. A few of the ways in which this has been described follow:

"It's hard to find the words to explain the power and love that I felt. There was total acceptance, and I somehow knew that I was exactly where I needed to be, doing exactly what I needed to be doing. I can write these words now as a memory of that experience, but the awareness of that experience while it was happening is something that I don't really think I'll ever be able to adequately describe."

"There just aren't human words enough to describe what I experienced. It was profound. I have made a poor attempt at describing it here."

"I don't really know how to explain what happened. I believe I was what they call 'born again.' It was an experience I will never forget. It has taught me that there is much, much more going on in life than we understand or know how to explain."

"I was enveloped in a warmth and a glow that I have never felt before. Suddenly, as this warmth spread out to my arms and limbs, I could see rays of golden light shooting out of my arms and hands. I just kept breathing, trying not to think, but to just feel. I was in such joy and peace that words are hard to describe it accurately."

3) The Experience Helps Sustain the Individual throughout the Rest of His or Her Life

Regardless of how many years have passed since the experience, participants often mention how their encounter helped to sustain them throughout many of life's ensuing challenges. The experience remains as clear as if it was yesterday. Many individuals become just as emotional discussing their story as they were when it happened. Because the memory of the experience remains so real, for many participants their encounter has provided them with an ongoing sense of hope, reassurance and encouragement:

"I was twelve years old when I had my personal encounter with the Divine. I did not have adult struggles or challenges at the time. I was an innocent child. However, as I grew and challenges and struggles seemed to find me, I was always able to look back on that experience (just as I am now) and find courage and the sense that there is more to life than my current situation. It has helped me many, many times."

"I never thought about *why* this happened until I had to answer this question. But I believe God made His existence known to me so I would remember his comforting presence when I would need it in the ensuing years. I have never been alone in life."

"The memory of that moment has been helpful to me during moments of loneliness, depression and sadness. It has been the one constant that has enabled me to pick myself up so that I could continue."

"Sometimes even I wonder: how do I continue to do it? How do I overcome the painful losses, the betrayals, the injustices, etc.? The only way I can answer this is to say that somewhere deep inside of me, I can now TRULY see and believe in the goodness of people and that all things have a purpose. It is that goodness that I choose to focus on in others, and it is that faith in some Universal meaning and connection with all things that keeps me believing. It has also helped to continue to have little glimpses of the Divine force that fortuitously comes into my life whenever I need a little boost or a little reality check . . . There is still much that I have yet to learn, but I guess if there wasn't, things might get quite boring."

4) The Experience Often Expands and Deepens the Individual's Faith

People from every imaginable faith and religious background inevitably mention how an encounter with the Divine has expanded their personal and religious beliefs. Conversely, individuals who once called themselves *atheist* or *agnostic* became quite certain of the reality of God after having a Divine encounter of their own. Oftentimes, because one's personal beliefs have broadened, individuals discuss the fact that they no longer see God as being confined to one religion but rather have a personal *knowing* that God is the God of all Creation. (See also "There is a sense of oneness," which follows below.) Because of their expanded beliefs, individuals who have experienced a personal encounter with the Divine often begin a spiritual search of their own, delving into other religions, other beliefs and other sources of truth.

Here are some of the ways that participants describe their personal faith and beliefs after having the experience:

"My spiritual belief system has been strengthened and fine-tuned by the encounters I've had with the Divine . . . I know that we create our own reality, that nothing happens by chance, and that Truth resides within each of us."

"I believe this experience has left me changed. I truly know that it has made me a more loving and patient person. My belief in the afterlife is much more than a belief—I now have a sense of knowing rather than believing."

"I know that my personal encounter has strengthened my belief in

Christ and in the spirit world. I now know that I exist and am able to be aware outside of my physical body. I'm truly grateful for that experience—I consider it an honor. Some may take it for granted, but I was raised in a very scientific and left-brained upbringing—an upbringing I took with me all through medical school. However, because of that experience, my perception has changed. Even during difficult times in the E.R., I can see each individual as a child of God, and I try to give that individual the patience, love and respect that a child of God deserves."

"I have become open-minded. I accept others for who and what they are and for what they believe. I no longer think of God as being judgmental. I no longer think of God as just being 'up there' in the sky. I now know that God is a part of us and we are a part of God."

"It has given me an inner strength and reinforced my expanded beliefs. There seems to be more for me to do. Meanwhile, I enjoy my garden and the moments God gives us."

"I see my spiritual life as being different before and after my experience. Before my experience, I was a faithful churchgoer, making an appearance just like you would punch the clock at work. Now, I still go to church, but I go because it allows me to take time out of my week to simply be in the presence of others who want to be in the presence of God. In addition to church, I also meditate. I also pray . . . and when I do go to church, I'm not just there—I'm there with the awareness that even if I don't always feel the presence of God, God can feel the presence of me."

"I can say that my God is a kind and loving God now. I no longer have to fear this idea of being sent straight to hell. The God I know and experienced is loving. He is forgiving. He gives you a chance to learn and grow, to pick yourself up from your mistakes . . . I have also learned that I can still have a personal interaction between God and myself; all I have to do is sit still and 'listen' within myself."

"I think the experience was brought to me to get me back on my path. What God's got in store for me, I just don't know, but I do know that I am supposed to keep learning and growing and keeping on keeping on . . . My experience with God was like being drowned in love, and I know I will never be the same again."

"I still consider myself a Christian, but I am much more of a Christian than the church I was brought up with. I can see the good in many religions. I can see how ultimately many religions are pointing to the same truth."

"To understand how my life has changed, let me tell you a story. I was brought up in the Charismatic Movement and often experienced the presence of the Holy Spirit and even 'speaking in tongues.' I felt at home in a Pentecostal church, where I met my husband and where I found many opportunities to be of service: teaching Sunday school, conducting children's church and teaching volunteer teachers how to teach.

"My experience raised questions for which my church had no answers. During my search for answers, a friend at my work introduced me to the Rosicrucians. Secretly, I became a member. During the long service at the Pentecostal church, I would sneak out and catch a subway train to the Rosicrucian Temple. With the group there, I learned to meditate and, surprisingly, to enjoy the viewpoints of all kinds of cultures and religions. The connection to all of humanity grew within me. My love for people expanded.

"One day, I was caught rushing back into church. My husband, standing outside the church looking for me, wanted to know 'Where were you?' He thought I had been working in the church office all those mornings. Replying to the question, I decided to say, 'If you really want to know, come with me next week.'

"The time came when we approached the Temple together. The building itself was unimpressive: gray painted brick, two stories, one door and a couple of windows. Nothing outside indicated what was inside. The only sign was a card propped up in the lower window: 'Library Hours,' it said. My husband looked surprised but said nothing. There was no objection to entering the darkened inner sanctuary with its

Egyptian motives. He listened with respect to the discussion afterwards at the table.

"We continued going together. In a short time we became more involved with the lessons. My husband became calmer and happier. For a Pentecostal man to become an occultist within the hour was nothing short of miraculous. One day I finally asked him why it had been so easy for him to make the transition. Then he told me that he had been standing in front of that same building a couple of years before he had even met me, handing out Gospel tracts. Inexplicably, he heard a voice behind him: 'These people will help you!' He spun around to look for the face of the one who had spoken, but there was only a plain gray building with a card in the window stating, 'Library Hours.'

"Since that time, we have been involved with Unity Church, the Edgar Cayce readings, exploring angels and even looking into UFO's, and Jesus still has a solid place in my heart . . . I feel as if my life of fifty-six years has actually been a continuous series of Divine encounters."

5) The Experiences Facilitates an Understanding That There Is a Reason for Everything; Life Becomes a Purposeful Experience

Individuals who have experienced a personal encounter with the Divine often describe how they now possess an understanding that life is truly purposeful. Perhaps, surprisingly, this understanding exists whether or not the individual has suffered a tragic loss or whether she or he has been forced to deal with even the most difficult challenges and experiences. The general sense is that the individual no longer feels victimized and that life is a process of personal growth and development. Repeatedly, these individuals might use a phrase such as "there is a reason for everything." Some of their comments follow:

"I strongly believe that everything occurring in our lives, even the most insignificant event, has a reason, a meaning and a purpose. Because we are souls in progress, all of our experiences are really opportunities for spiritual development. We are the ones that see these things as obstacles in life."

"It helped me to feel worthwhile. It helped me to handle the things I was going through. It helped me to understand that most of these challenges have happened to help me grow and become a better person. In fact, the person I've become and am still in the process of becoming is because of my life's experiences and my personal encounter with God."

"I have begun to feel grateful for everything in life (see 1Thes. 5:18), and even now, several times each day, I express my gratitude to God."

"I believe we are all here for a purpose. I believe that we are guided by spirit to find that purpose if we simply remain open to it . . . It is a shame that so much of organized religion seems to divide individuals rather than bring them together. Perhaps it is similar to my still having a stubborn attachment to my current state of being, when I know there is much more. I think that as we find our true purpose, our sense of how that fits in to the rest of humankind becomes much clearer."

"I thank God for each day, no matter what happens. I now know how to keep going against all odds. I may not always win, but I know I will never lose. I have many, many blessings, even in the midst of life's challenges."

"In terms of how I have grown, it has become apparent to me that even if my life appears to be falling apart, that is due only to the perception of my finite mind and not the truth. All things are in Divine Order, whether we choose to see it that way or not . . . I don't imagine that chicks have a good time hatching out of their shells either."

"From this experience, I have also learned that whatever any one person is subjected to is exactly what Spirit believes that person needs for soul growth. I have learned that out of adversity and illness can come amazing strength . . . I used to be an obsessive planner with lists (and lists that had lists); now I have learned that you need to live each day for the present moment. I have also learned that love and caring are the foremost priorities in my life."

"I believe there are no accidents . . . I believe in reincarnation, karma, the brotherhood of humankind and that someday we will all come to this same stage of realization. No one is lost. We're all on the same path; we're just at varying stages of that path. One who is ahead is no better than one who is farther behind, any more than an eleven-year-old is better than a six-year-old."

6) There Is a Sense of Oneness; There Is a Profound Sense of Connection with the Universe, with Others and with One's Surroundings

The overall philosophy detailed by individuals who have had an experience with the Divine might best be expressed as a consciousness of oneness. Participants often describe the fact that one of the most profound and memorable aspects of their experience was feeling connected with the universe, with others and with all surroundings. They generally describe feeling as if they were a part of everything—a part of God, a part of nature, a part of others. This feeling also seems to entail the awareness that "everything is part of God." Because of this sense of oneness and the awareness that God is in all things, frequently participants no longer feel disconnected from others, and any previous animosity or judgment is quickly set aside.

Another aspect connected with this thematic element is the fact that individuals often describe how their understanding of religion has changed and expanded to include a reverence and respect for all other beliefs and faiths:

"I have overcome judgmental attitudes. I was raised with attitudes of racism, anti-Catholicism, and dim views of those who did not go to church, raise their children in a certain way or observe the 'proper' sex-role mandates. I was also trained to think ill of those who gambled, lied and cheated. My experience has enabled me to overcome all of these misperceptions."

"All at once I had the awesome realization that I was, and am, united with all that there is—all humanity, all animate and inanimate objects. I felt the presence of this Life flowing through the sky, the trees, the yard, everything around me. I became aware of the fact that this same Life force flowed through me. In those moments I knew with absolute certainty that I was not alone and that the Divine had an ongoing place in our lives."

"I no longer believe that God belongs to a particular religion. I believe that God cares individually for everyone and everything in his creation. I believe that we are all one and that as we grow into an understanding of this universal law, the earth will become a better place."

"I felt totally connected with the entire universe. I felt a powerful oneness with God. My entire being resonated with the wonder and joy of Life. I now know that the Divine light is in all of us and we need to learn to respect that light in others."

"I believe in the Oneness of all things. I know that this is a loving universe and it's only getting better. There is an upswelling of spiritual consciousness among all people that is wonderful. I feel that we are being made ready for something tremendous. What a terrific time to be alive!"

"I now have an insatiable passion to continue on my spiritual journey toward God, our Creator . . . I believe that there are as many paths to God as there are people, and in their own way they are all valid. I know that in the end, everything that is and all that can ever be will become a part of God."

"We are all swimming in a pool of God. God is everywhere. We can continue to allow religion to hold our understanding back, but when we combine it with spirituality, the picture becomes much broader. God is an all-loving God. God has not given up on any part of his creation. (Remember the parable of the ninety-nine sheep? God is always going after that last sheep!) We are all destined to be a part of God."

"Today, I guess I would have to say that I find much of organized religion distasteful. Inevitably, they follow rules, regulations and ideas that were devised by human beings. Too often these rules and ideas have created every imaginable human grief and suffering . . . my personal perception is now one in which I strive to see the Creator in all that has been created. For all of us, regardless of our beliefs, we are slowly moving toward the One who created each and every one of us. When organized religion understands that, we might truly have 'peace on earth, good will toward all men.'"

7) The Experience Entails the Presence of a Love That Is Indescribable

Individuals who experience a personal encounter with a Divine presence frequently describe that it felt like being in the presence of love. It is a love that is hard to describe to others—it seems to consist of an energy that fills the recipient's entire being. Participants generally state that it felt like an unconditional love that they had never experienced before. In many instances, there is almost a melancholy realization that this depth of unconditional love may never be experienced again—at least not while on the earth. During the encounter, individuals feel a sense of total acceptance and understanding; there is never any indication of condemnation or judgment.

That total sense of unconditional love, acceptance and non-judgment was perhaps best expressed by an eighty-three-year-old woman who stated that after the experience she frequently found herself questioning, "Why is it so hard for people to understand that an all-loving God would love everyone and that a God who loves everyone would create a plan that enabled everyone to make it?"

"For once in my life I felt really loved—like I mattered to someone . . . To know that the Almighty loves me, loves me, has been the greatest thing I've received in all of my life. I also know that He loves us all . . . Since that time, I have learned to love myself."

"I continue to be incredibly blessed. My life has become a living testimony to the blessings that Spirit provides for us. Because I experienced being loved unconditionally, I have tried to learn how to love unconditionally in return."

"Even though I was raised to know of an afterlife with God, I could never and will never again experience the depth of emotion of joy again until I die. There is no doubt in my mind that life does not end at the end of this one."

"I finally got it. The person I needed to love most of all was me. I had finally felt a love that I needed to feel toward myself."

"I knew that this love that was coming in on me was the same love that was being sent to everyone and every living creature. There was no difference. I also knew that this was the ultimate love in the universe and that much of what man perceives as love is simply a shadow by comparison."

"At the time of my experience, I was walking through life like a zombie. I now feel that my assignment, if you will, is to learn how to love everyone with the same measure of love that I felt. I have come a long way in that endeavor, but I still have a long way to go. But I know what God's presence feels like, and I want to be able to share that same love in return."

8) There Is an Awareness That God Has an Ongoing Concern for Us

In addition to feeling a depth of love that has not been experienced previously, an individual who has undergone a personal encounter with the Divine is apt to describe how he or she is now quite confident that God is personally aware of each and every human being. Not only does the participant describe this awareness but also the fact that God seems to possess a concern for His or Her creation. In addition, the participant often possesses an accompanying belief that God truly has a plan or a mission in mind that the individual is best able to perform. There seems to be an awareness that God has an ongoing presence in all of Creation:

"I'm still comfortable saying that I am a Catholic, but now I am also a student of metaphysics. I am still eager to learn and explore. I am open to all philosophical teachings. I have learned to accept truth, wherever I find it . . . My encounter made me known to God, and He became personally known to me. If there had ever been any doubt as to the reality of His existence, it was eradicated in that experience. If I could capture those emotions and feelings again, I would be forever grateful—it would be like drinking from the Holy Grail!"

"I remain a work in progress, and I suppose I'm beginning to feel more comfortable with that idea. I am working at following the plan that God seems to have in mind for me . . . Through my work, it seems that countless miracles have happened in individuals' lives. The feedback I have received in terms of my helpfulness to others has given me a sense of encouragement and a sense of responsibility—responsibility to use the gifts I have been given in a loving and caring way."

"It has taught me that God lives and RULES!"

"I have learned that God loves and knows me."

"I know that this experience happened to let me know that I was not alone, that there was more to this world than what I realized and that I was being supported and loved . . . I know that we are all loved unconditionally. We are also supported and guided every moment. We are also one with God. When I gained this awareness, it was the beginning of true perception.

9) During the Experience, Everything Stands Still—There Is the Absence of Sound, Space and Time

Oftentimes individuals who have an experience with the Divine describe how for a moment or for a fraction of an instant everything stands completely still. It seems as if they have somehow entered a dimension or a vacuum in which there in no time and no space. Everything is motionless. Somehow in this state they become completely focused on and aware of only the experience they are involved with. Even in the midst of noise, commotion or other people, for a fleeting fraction of time, participants are convinced that the universe stood still and everything became frozen in place. Some of the ways in which individuals have described this phenomenon are as follows:

"It was as if everything became frozen in place. I could hear no sound and see no movement around me. There in the garden I felt totally connected with the entire Universe. I felt a powerful oneness with God. My entire being resonated with the wonder and joy of Life."

"I remember that I was sitting there being very quiet. There was complete silence around me—even the insects were still. I was watching the setting sun, and it seemed much more fascinating than I had ever noticed before. I became very focused on what I was witnessing."

"It was not my imagination. I was speechless; it was like the whole Universe stood still."

"One moment there was noise all around. There were music, people's voices, and normal sounds like you would hear in a restaurant. In the next moment everything became silent. I suddenly realized that everything was completely and totally still."

"I was working in my small garden and was lifting the shovel to turn over a pile of earth. I had been under a great deal of stress and was doing the yard work to relax—it also needed to be done. Suddenly, I experienced complete and total stillness:

"It was as if everything became frozen in place. I could hear no sound and see no movement around me. There in the garden I felt totally connected with the entire Universe. I felt a powerful oneness with God. My entire being resonated with the wonder and joy of Life."

"I can still remember the feeling of somehow being lifted and briefly taken out of time. As I recall, it seems like there was also an absence of all sound. The moment also seemed longer than it could have been. I didn't see anything, but I know that I experienced Divine intervention—without it, I know I would have been killed or seriously injured."

■

Each of these thematic elements is descriptive in terms of the variety of ways individuals experienced their personal encounter with the Divine, as well as the aftereffects of that experience. Perhaps, inevitably, there will be individuals who will not perceive some of the accounts of contemporary encounters with the Divine contained within this volume as valid experiences with God, spirit or some kind of Divine presence. However, without exception, there was never any question in the minds of the contributors as to the validity of their experience. Quite a few individuals used the phrase "I know what I saw" when describing their encounter. In many instances, the encounter provided the impetus of change that has remained with the individual even decades later. Some found a faith, when they had none. Many who had been in the midst of confusion felt somehow enlightened. Those who were depressed or saddened felt comforted. A number discussed how the experience suddenly eradicated fears that had troubled them all of life. Individuals who were overwhelmed by life's challenges, no matter how large or small, felt the presence of something much greater than self ease their burden.

It is interesting to note that in his 1923 classic, *Cosmic Consciousness*, Dr. Richard Maurice Bucke proposed that many of these experiences suggested that humankind was simply in the process of a consciousness evolution. With this in mind, Bucke predicted that these experiences would eventually become more typical and ordinary in the course of human life. In fact, Bucke believed that "Cosmic Consciousness" would ultimately give birth to a new world view and even a new level of human creature prone to these types of experiences. In describing the impact this would have on the rest of humankind, Bucke theorized:

> **The human soul will be revolutionized . . . The evidence of immortality will live in every heart as sight in every eye. Doubt of God and of eternal life will be as impossible as is now doubt of existence; the evidence of each will be the**

> same . . . Churches, priests, forms, creeds, prayers, all agents, all intermediaries between the individual [hu]man and God will be permanently replaced by direct unmistakable intercourse. Sin will no longer exist nor will salvation be desired. Men[/women] will not worry about death or a future, about the kingdom of heaven, about what may come with and after the cessation of the life of the present body. Each soul will feel and know itself to be immortal, will feel and know that the entire universe with all its good and with all its beauty is for it and belongs to it forever. The world peopled by men [individuals] possessing cosmic consciousness will be as far removed from the world of today as this is from the world as it was before the advent of self-consciousness.
>
> Buck, 5

What if it was truly understood that there were innumerable ways for individuals to experience their own encounters with the Divine? What might happen to our collective worldview if we suddenly realized that, in truth, there was a Creator inextricably connected to all that had been created? Perhaps these stories suggest that the time has come for even a twenty-first century world to acknowledge that there may be much more to us than simply a physical body. Perhaps the time has come to acknowledge that we can never really be alone.

References and Recommended Reading

Bucke, Richard Maurice, M.D. *Cosmic Consciousness: A Study in the Evolution of the Human Mind*. New York: E.P. Dutton and Company, Inc. 1923.

Burtt, E.A., editor. *The Teachings of the Compassionate Buddha*. New York: Mentor (Penguin Group). 1982.

Carty, Rev. Charles Mortimer. *Padre Pio: The Stigmatist*. St. Paul, Minnesota: Radio Replies Press. 1963.

Chetanananda, Swami. *Vivekananda: East Meets West*. St. Louis, Missouri: Vedanta Society of St. Louis. 1995.

Clark, Glenn, Glenn Harding, and Starr Daily. *The Third Front: Through the Paths of Faith, Hope and Love*. St Paul, Minnesota: Macalester Park Publishing Co. 1944.

A Course in Miracles. New York City: Foundation for Inner Peace. 1975.

Daily, Starr. *Love Can Open Prison Doors*. San Gabriel, California: Willing Publishing Company. 1954.

Daily, Starr. *Release*. New York: Harper & Brothers Publishers. 1942.

DeBecker, Raymond. *The Understanding of Dreams and Their Influence on the History of Man*. New York: Hawthorn Books, Inc. 1968.

The Duchess of St. Albans. *Magic of a Mystic: Stories of Pablo Pio*. New York: Clarkson N. Potter, Inc. 1983.

Esslemont, J.E. *Bahá'u'lláh and the New Era*. Wilmette, Illinois: BaháI Publishing Trust. 1980.

Fayed, Ahmed A. "Another Sphinx Mystery." *Venture Inward* magazine. Virginia Beach, VA: Association for Research and Enlightenment, Inc. May/June 1998

Irving, Washington. *Life of Mahomet*. New York: E.P. Dutton and Company, Inc. 1915.

James, William. *The Varieties of Religious Experience*. New York: Modern Library. 1936.

The Holy Bible, King James Version, 1979.

Isaac, Stephen. *Songs from the House of Pilgrimage*. Boston: Branden Press. 1971.

The Jewish Encyclopedia: A Descriptive Record of the History, Religion, Literature, and Customs of the Jewish People from the Earliest Times to the Present Day. London: Funk and Wagnalls Co. 1901.

Lonnerstrand, Sture. *I Have Lived Before: The True Story of the Reincarnation of Shanti Devi*. Huntsville, Arkansas: Ozark Mountain Publishers. 1998.

Moody, Raymond A. Jr., M.D. *Life After Life*. New York: Bantam Books. 1977.

Newhouse, Flower A. *Here Are Your Answers (Volume III)*. Escondido, CA: Christward Ministry. 1983.

Newhouse, Flower A. *Insights into Reality*. Escondido, CA: Christward Ministry. 1975.

Newhouse, Flower A. *Rediscovering the Angels*. Escondido, CA: Christward Ministry. 1976.

Nikhilananda, Swami. *Vivekananda: A Biography*. Calcutta: Advaita Ashrama. 1982.

Paramananda, Swami, translator. *Srimad-Bhagavad-Gita*. Cohasset, MA: Vedanta Centre. 1974.

Parente, Fr. Alessio, O.F.M., Cap. *"Send Me Your Guardian Angel" Padre Pio*. Amsterdam, NY: The Noteworthy Co. 1983.

Pickthall, Marmaduke William M., translator. *The Holy Qur'aan*. Elmhurst, NY: Tahrike Tarsile Quran, Inc. 1997.

Prabhavananda, Swami, and Frederick Manchester. *The Upanishads*. New York: Mentor (Penguin Group). 1975.

Puryear, Herbert B., Ph.D. "Ye Must Be Born Again," public lecture. Companion tape to Chapter 4, *Why Jesus Taught Reincarnation*. Scottsdale, Arizona. ca. 1993.

Rawat, Kirti S. "Shanti Devi's Past Lives." *Venture Inward* magazine. Virginia Beach, VA: Association for Research and Enlightenment, Inc. March/April 1997.

Smith, Joseph, translator. *The Book of Mormon*. Salt Lake City, Utah: The Church of Jesus Christ of Latter-day Saints. 1950.

Tweedie, Irina. *The Chasm of Fire*. Great Britain: Element Books. 1993.

Tweedie, Irina. *Daughter of Fire*. Grass Valley, California: Blue Dolphin Publishing, Inc. 1986.

Van de Castle, Robert L. Ph.D. *Our Dreaming Mind*. New York: Ballantine Books. 1994.

Vaughan-Lee, Llewellyn. *The Lover and the Serpent*. Great Britain: Element Books. 1990.

Waite, Arthur Edward, and W.P. Swainson. *Three Famous Mystics: Saint-Martin, Jacob Boehme, Swedenborg*. London: Rider & Co. n.d.

Yogananda, Paramahansa. *Autobiography of a Yogi*. Los Angeles: Self-Realization Fellowship. 1994.

4TH DIMENSION PRESS

An Imprint of A.R.E. Press

4th Dimension Press is an imprint of A.R.E. Press, the publishing division of Edgar Cayce's Association for Research and Enlightenment (A.R.E.).

We publish books, DVDs, and CDs in the fields of intuition, psychic abilities, ancient mysteries, philosophy, comparative religious studies, personal and spiritual development, and holistic health.

For more information, or to receive a catalog, contact us by mail, phone, or online at:

4th Dimension Press
215 67th Street
Virginia Beach, VA 23451-2061
800-333-4499

4THDIMENSIONPRESS.COM